OFFICE
HOUR

**Fresh Corporate Environments
from Around the Globe**

GINGKO PRESS

OFFICE HOUR

**Fresh Corporate Environments
from Around the Globe**

ISBN: 978-1-58423-476-0

First Published in the United States of America by Gingko Press
by arrangement with Sandu Publishing Co., Limited

Gingko Press, Inc.
1321 Fifth Street
Berkeley, CA 94710 USA
Tel: (510) 898 1195
Fax: (510) 898 1196
Email: books@gingkopress.com
www.gingkopress.com

Copyright © 2011 by SANDU PUBLISHING

Sponsored by: Design 360° – Concept and Design Magazine
Chief Editor: Wang Shaoqiang
Executive Editor: Sasha Lo
Chief Designer: Wang Shaoqiang
Book Designer: Antiny Wu
Sales Managers:
Niu Guanghui (China), Daniela Huang (International)
Address:
3rd Floor, West Tower,
No.10 Ligang Road, Haizhu District,
510280, Guangzhou, China
Tel: (86)-20-84344460
Fax: (86)-20-84344460
sandu.sales@gmail.com
www.sandu360.com

Cover project by Maurice Mentjens Design

Printed and bound in China

PREFACE

Jaspar Jansen
Jeroen Dellensen
i29 | interior architects

In a book full of amazing projects it is easy to celebrate the creativity of architects and designers and the powerful images that are produced, but maybe we should start at the beginning.

When designing an office, more than with other spaces, functionality and efficiency seem to be of importance. After all it is where business is done. Work is largely about producing something (whether it is a service or a product) and making a profit with it. And as we all know you only make a profit if there is a good balance between time and money invested and the quality and price of the result. Functionality and efficiency are important tools to reach this.

One way to approach this functionality is to think of the route and the positioning of different areas. For instance you can arrange it in a way so that there is very little social space and therefore people stay at their desks and work harder. Or you can choose to arrange the space in a way that encourages people to meet so creative interaction is encouraged. An example of efficiency could be to spend as little money as possible on the interior and get cheap or recycled furniture so the company can stay financially and geographically flexible. On the other hand if you really invest in the interior you may retain your employees longer. If you get nice furniture people will be more likely to spend longer, more comfortable hours using that furniture.

These are obviously black and white examples and often we strive for the best of both worlds. Nevertheless practical decisions like this have to be carefully made. You could argue that these decisions are not made solely by the architect but rather by the client, and this is certainly true, since the client should be the source from which objectives are received. But it is our experience that not many clients have a strict, written-down program of how the physical "business" should be organized. They enter a new building, or have one built for them, and they are exposed to endless possibilities. Making decisions is basically a creative process where trained creatives can be of help. And even when we have this program it doesn't tell us how things will look! Materials, color, and the spatial experience are all defined by organizational choices. During this process, the company identity is refined.

The amazing thing is that often when we start to answer questions about what this experience should be and what the theme or underlying pattern is, problems that were first only practical and functional get solved in a very natural way. To our great satisfaction often we see that all details organically fall into place and become an inseparable whole. We look for choices that solve multiple challenges at the same time. They have to tell a conceptual story about the company, the space and the users of the space. Decisions about specific functional issues need to be integrated into a final result. A smart architectural design not only serves a practical purpose, but also advertises the company as a powerful image.

An individual is defined by his characteristics, but sometimes different unique individuals have characteristics in common. This is how we view design. No characteristics are exclusive, but in combination they create a personality. And as with people's personalities, the more clearly just one or a few details stand out, the more powerful the personality. In order to create a strong design, a strong image has to be envisioned. People need to be able to identify with this image in a positive way – especially the people who work in the space. The goal is for people to feel happy and proud working in their designed environment.

Within these pages, you will encounter a selection of the finest designed offices and work spaces all around the world.

CONTENTS

Design | FORM US WITH LOVE
design studio
Client | FORM US WITH LOVE
design studio
Photography | Jonas Lindström
Area | 200 sqm
Location | Stockholm, Sweden

FUWL STUDIO

With the new studio at Sankt Eriksgatan 106, FORM US WITH LOVE design studio intends to create a vibrant space for design in Stockholm. FUWL plans for exhibitions, lectures and a pop-up shop.

The design studio is divided into three levels: office, studio and workshop. The interior will be completed in October 2011 and is inspired by the gallery world mixed with industrial facilities and Lego.

The effort has been made possible with the help of partners within the design and architecture sector.

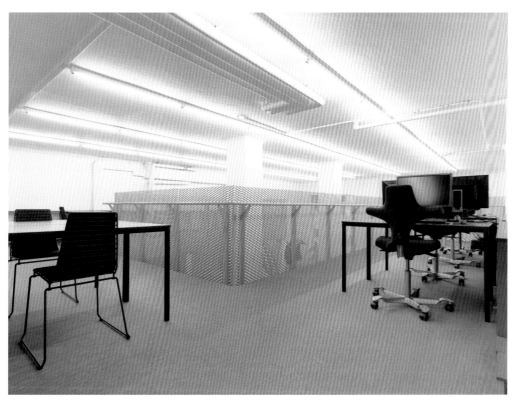

Design | studioquint and Jos Roodbol
Client | University Amsterdam
Photography | Mark Weemen
Area | 275 sqm
Location | Amsterdam, the Netherlands

nextdoor

Nextdoor is a temporary interior design for the Centre of Amsterdam School of Entrepreneurship (CASE). CASE is a part of the University of Amsterdam. Following a new educational program students of different fields get the opportunity here to start up their own business and develop a business concept and market strategy with the support of the university. The brief contained 10 permanent work-units and 40 flexible work areas. The budget for renovating this 275 sqm office space was extremely tight. Therefore, all furniture and work-units have been assembled by low cost standard door elements. By taking out the ceiling the structure of the existing building has been made visible. The starting point of the spatial intervention was based on the specific programmatic conditions. Every student has to develop his own business identity and at the same time has to orient himself in a complex economical network. The work-units are white cubes. Differentiation has been achieved by adding different interior elements made by black plywood, offering the necessary storage spaces and stabilizing the units and introducing a new layer of scale. By a linear placing of the units a long-drawn working object appears, creating a spatial zoning. The interior of the working object turns into a kaleidoscopic inner world that enables concentrated work possibilities.

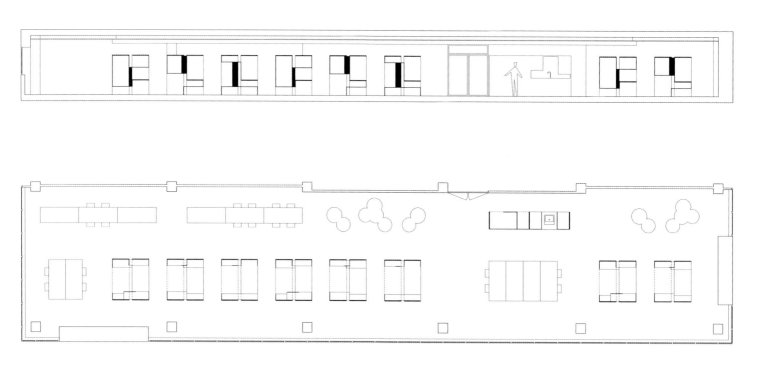

Design | nendo
Client | nendo
Photography | Daici Ano
Area | 132 sqm
Location | Tokyo, Japan

meguro office

nendo's office is located near the Meguro River in Tokyo, on the fifth floor of an old office building. They wanted the usual spaces and functions – meeting space, management, workspace and storage to be separate, but also to maintain a sense of connection between them. To achieve this effect, they divided the space with walls that seem to sag and flop like a piece of cloth held up between two hands, enclosing the various spaces more than the usual office dividers, but less than actual walls. Employees can move between spaces by walking over the parts of the walls that "sag" the most, thus emphasizing the contrast between

the use of different spaces. Spaces that need more sound-proofing are enclosed with the kind of plastic curtains you might find at a small factory so that people can work without worrying about noise but not feel isolated. When one stands up and looks through the whole space, people, shelves and plants seem to appear and disappear as if floating between the waves.

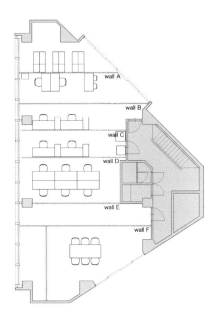

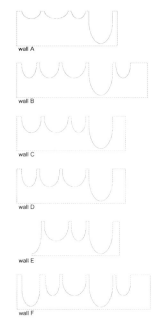

138.18㎡   PLAN 1:150

ELEVATION 1:150

Design | Origins Architecture
Client | Onesize
Photography | Stijn Poelstra
Area | 300 sqm
Location | Amsterdam, the Netherlands

Onesize interior

The client, a motion graphics designer from Onesize, needed dark spaces for projection and studio work. The visual modeling work that is done in the studio inspired Origins Architecture to make an object with a minimal of polygons, transforming the program into an interesting shape and in the meantime subdividing the space for a clear routing.

The architects used low grade spruce multiplex better known as underlayment which is usually used under carpeting. Besides the cost issue they strongly believed that the juxtaposition of high definition detailing and a low grade material would make both stand out better. This contrast is also echoed in the relation between the existing building and the central sculptural shape: wood & concrete, detail and material, dark & light.

The architects hoped to create an interesting and intriguing space with minimal means. They started out with more complex shapes, but the simpler they became the better the result. The architecture office specializes in sustainable building, so they were also keeping an eye on the environmental impact. By doing so they actually came up with a sculptural volume that hardly has any losses in the making. The most important result is that the interior really fits the client, both in terms of program and in appearance.

1. projector

2. classic mac

3. classic camera

4. 8mm editor

5. paintgun

6. toy robot

7. film rolls

8. camera`s

9. 3x joysticks

10. atari console

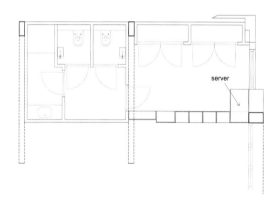

server

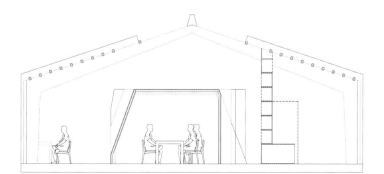

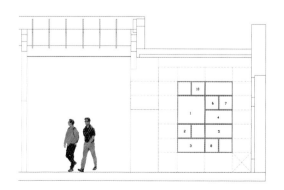

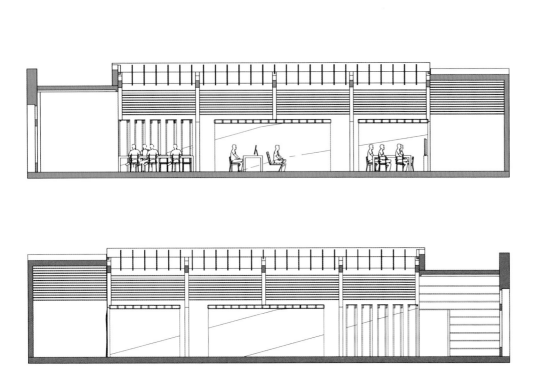

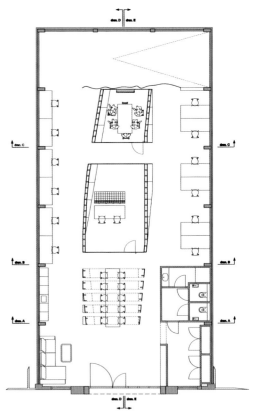

Design | Studio Joost van Bleiswijk
Client | Nothing
Photography | Joachim Baan
Area | 100 sqm
Location | Amsterdam, the Netherlands

Nothing cardboard office interior

Nothing is an Amsterdam-based, independent entrepreneurial agency that delivers innovation and commercial creativity for local and international clients out of a cardboard box. Literally. The Nothing office, built entirely of cardboard, was designed by internationally recognized designers Joost van Bleiswijk and Alrik Koudenburg.

Alrik Koudenburg came up with the idea to use cardboard to do the complete interior. He presented a total concept to his client and they had the guts and trust to take it on. The structure is made out of a variety of volumes and houses all the activities of the agency. It has a boardroom, a grand elevated office and a library work area. And it's freestanding – one could completely walk around it, over it, or work inside it.

Alrik Koudenburg and Joost van Bleiswijk created a variety of spaces: a coffee corner, boardroom, brainstorm area with meeting table and book cabinet, desks, elevated work space and a storage room – in a 100 square meter office. The result is a peaceful décor that inspires and provides a homelike atmosphere.

The use of the 'No Screw, No Glue' technique on this scale was never explored before and the strong lines allowed Joost to apply details, volumes and furniture. The designers used more than 500m^2 of the most 'Nothing-building material' they could find – reinforced cardboard. It was CNC-cut and left the team with 1500 elements that they could slot together without the need of screws or glue.

Design | i29 interior architects
Client | Gummo
Photography | i29 interior architects
Area | 450 sqm
Location | Amsterdam, the Netherlands

recycled office

As Gummo was only going to be renting the space on the first floor of the old Parool newspaper building in Amsterdam for two years, i29 convinced Gummo to embrace the mantra of "reduce, reuse, recycle" to create a stylish office space that would have the least possible impact on the environment and their wallets. They developed a theme that reflects Gummo's personality and design philosophy – simple, uncomplicated, no-nonsense, yet unquestionably stylish with a twist of humour. Everything in the office conforms to the new house style of white and grey. All the furniture was locally sourced via Marktplaats (the Dutch eBay), charity shops and whatever was left over at the old office. Everything was then spray painted with polyurea Hotspray (an environmentally friendly paint) to conform to the new color scheme. Even Jesus wasn't immune, as you can see in the pictures. The new office is a perfect case study of a smart way to fill a temporary space stylishly and at minimal cost. The collection of old and repaired products in its new coating has given a new potential and soul to the old furniture.

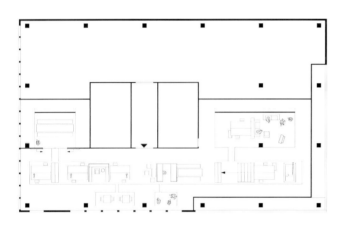

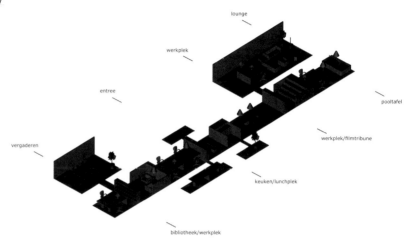

Design | CoudamyDesign
Client | Elegangz
Photography | Benjamin Boccas
Area | 180 sqm
Location | Paris, France

Cardboard Office

The task was to convert the 160m^2 empty industrial space into an operational working space for the 20 employees with an original design able to transmit a young and dynamic image. Budget was restricted to the minimum and timing was only 5 weeks from concept to realization.

The whole design was completed with 4cm thick water-resistant honeycomb cardboard. Even if it is a packaging product it is a cheap, green and technical material offering many advantages to traditional building materials. Everything was mounted with a system of folding combined with glue and tape; no additional structures were added. Lightness, compression resistance, and easy cutting made the cardboard a solution to build everything in seven days. Shelves are made of stacked pieces of cardboard to get a strong structure; thanks to the angled cuts system, partitions are stable and can be oriented in many directions; the meeting cabin was built with honeycomb resistance only with cutting, glue and tape. Lighting was done with an old stock of white umbrellas hung upside down, which diffuses the light to provide a soft lighting.

Based on reuse, low-tech and indirect elements, this unusual interior design offers a functional and flexible space, which could be built in a very short time for a competitive price. A mix of soft and poetic umbrellas was hung in the industrial warehouse. The contrast between rugged rock wall and fragile cardboard gives a unique spirit to the office, conveying the client's dynamic image.

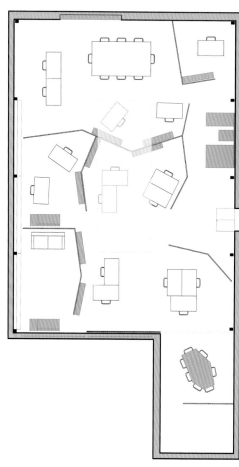

Design I DESPACHO COUPE S.L.P.
Client I DESPACHO COUPE S.L.P.
Photography I Miguel de Guzmán
Area I 33.45 sqm
Location I Toledo, Spain

ARCHITECTURAL OFFICE

An office is a desk.

The premises, where the action is performed, are in Toledo's old quarter. The site is one meter above a tiny square and connected to it by steps.

In the first stage, the task was stripping the place, which was originally a carpenter's workshop, of every minor element: suspended ceilings, partition walls, and coverings. By using a large glass door the architects open the space towards the square. The office will become integrated in the town and the floor will be at the viewer's eye level. Finally, the space and its façade is turned into a single entity through the grey color.

The second step is designing a building inside of the first one. The architects will need nothing more than a desk and some shelves, the bigger the better. The furniture is the outcome of a single profile made to work, with no differences or rank. It could be any size, but it is as big as the space it is set in allows. The furniture has its own flooring, and all the necessary appliances for its use. On a wooden framework, a translucent methacrylate plate with a satin sheen was placed. This condenses the light, casts no shadows and permits seeing the structure and the objects in it.

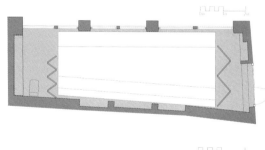

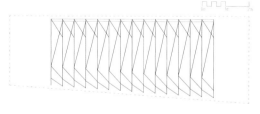

Design | TERVHIVATAL
Client | Benedict & Helfer
Photography | Tamás BUJNOVSZKY ©
Area | 290 sqm
Location | Budapest, Hungary

Goldberger loft office

The space has been divided into smaller offices and meeting rooms using plaster-board boxes on steel frames. These boxes were slightly elevated and the spaces between the boxes serve the purpose of hallways. The boxes are either attached to the floor or are floating. The counter-arched ceiling provides a contrast between the boxes.

Hidden LED-lighting is used to illuminate these box-like structures, which have been installed under the cubes. The space can also be used as a club venue at night. For using the office space as a club, a separate bar with a service counter has been created.

The floors of the box-interiors are covered in grey linoleum and the entire hall is polished concrete.

The inner height of the loft space is about five meters. The client wanted separate rooms for the different working stations. They do internet advertising and all kinds of graphic and advertising jobs. There is a department of programmers, another one for graphic work, and so on. The clients needed separate places for different kind of works but they hated the usual office buildings with plasterboard partitions and small rooms. They wanted something extraordinary.

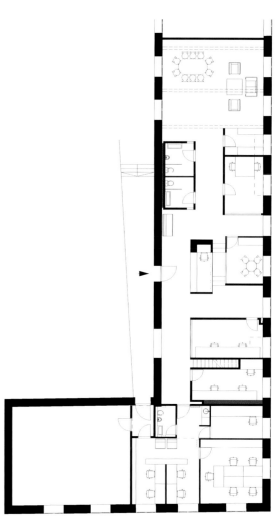

Design | Corvin Cristian
Client | Headvertising
Photography | Vlad Caprarescu
Area | 400 sqm
Location | Bucharest, Romania

Headvertising

Inside the former Romanian Stock Exchange, the shipping crates themed furniture acts as storage, movable dividing walls, dynamic company statement and reverence on the genius loci. The over sized lamps and the chesterfields add a homey feeling to the otherwise austere design. The warmth is brought by the natural touch of plywood.

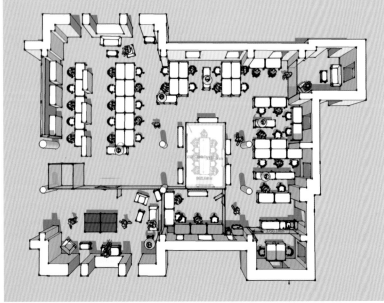

Design | Mathieu Lehanneur
Client | JWT
Photography | Véronique Huyghes
Area | 1,000 sqm
Location | Paris, France

The JWT Agency

Perpetually on the lookout for new ways to live, sleep, create and work, Mathieu Lehanneur turns the advertising agency JWT (Neuilly/Seine) into a "digital plant station", a new reflection from the designer about contemporary working styles and the necessary invented depictions of them when applied to the professional world of communications. First symbolic move: to reverse the usual dynamic of authority by placing the two chairmen and the director of JWT on the ground floor, as close as possible to the hub of the agency, separated from the reception simply by tall doors. The second meaningful gesture is that the agency's specific digital sensibility is entirely embodied by the meeting room, transformed into a creative cavern with walls totally made from paper fiber, "It has literally sucked up and recycled the available paper in the agency, an archaic and useless support that JWT France eventually envisions totally eliminating." Providing excellent soundproofing, usually used for thermal insulation in organic buildings, the final execution sublimates the irregular exterior surface, a shell whose spray projects neo-archaism contrasts with the milky and luminous purity of the internal shell: pure James Bond genius where the most unobtrusive rock hides Dr No's ultra technical trace.

Design | Kamat & Rozario Architecture
Client | Ananya Technologies
Photography | Smruti Kamat
Area | 3,000 sqft
Location | Bangalore, India

Ananya Technologies Pvt Ltd

The plan of the space was conceived as an integrated circuit board, which was an integral part of the client's products. The color-coded pipes crisscrossing the ceiling connect various hubs in the space and are reminiscent of the tracks in a circuit board. The pipes travel along the ceiling and vertically along walls to create a 3-dimensional idea of the circuit board and simultaneously double up as electrical conduits. The colored pipes in the ceiling also helped in circumventing

a false ceiling thereby reducing the cost significantly.

The architects decided to lift the storage off from the floor and inhabit the space below it. A conference room was created below a metal storage loft hanging from the ceiling. A corrugated MS sheet was suspended from the slab to serve as storage. This served a number of functions – a large amount of floor space got freed up, and the volume of the conference room was reduced

enough for efficient air conditioning. It also avoided huge amounts of cabinetry.

The same language translates into other parts of the design as well. For instance, the visual barrier in the work stations was made from the same sheet.

The wooden fan blades in the entrance area were made to be reminiscent of old aircraft blades.

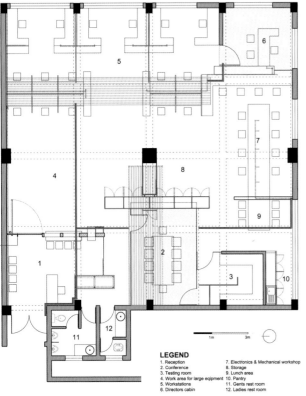

LEGEND
1. Reception
2. Conference
3. Testing room
4. Work area for large eqipment
5. Workstations
6. Directors cabin
7. Electronics & Mechanical workshop
8. Storage
9. Lunch area
10. Pantry
11. Gents rest room
12. Ladies rest room

1m   3m

Design | za bor architects
Client | za bor achitects
Photography | Peter Zaytsev
Area | 76 sqm
Location | Moscow, Russia

za bor architects office

The office of the za bor architects is situated in an outbuilding that used to be the kitchen-factory of the First State bearing plant. When the architects started to reconstruct the main building of the complex, a half-ruined four-storey construction erected back in 1932, they had to spend a lot of time onsite, so they moved from Sadovaya to Sharikopodshipnikovskaya Street and made a new office in one of the outbuildings in the factory-kitchen complex courtyard.

While creating their own office, the architects decided to fully use the industrial aesthetics of the complex: in the former storehouse the old brickwork was revealed and whitewashed; the original wooden beams were painted in grey – one of the basic colors of the office. Frameworks for the furniture and places for meeting clients were made from rough steel channel profiles and I-beams used for the reconstruction of the building.

The dominating structure of the office is a bright yellow construction that has become the main sight of za bor style. The lavatory and the shower room dressed in grey ceramic granite are hidden behind the yellow wall.

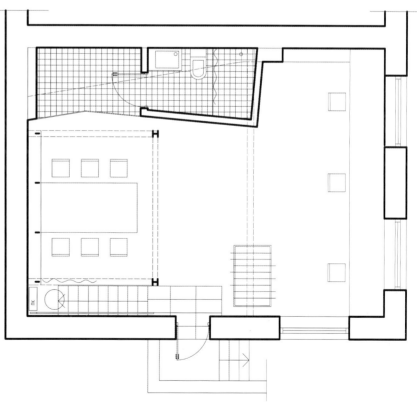

Design | arquitectura x
Client | Ruales Izurieta Publicidad
Photography | Sebastian Crespo
Area | 82 sqm
Location | Quito, Ecuador

RI offices

This small intervention for a young publicity agency is based on the need for flexible, adaptable and expandable space for their multiple tasks and changing needs, within a very low budget, since a large investment had to be made on hardware, software and specialized photographic, film and editing equipment. Parallel to cost reduction the scheme had to provide a strong and fresh image to the agency as this was their first formal office; the architect's response was to remove all the standard anodyne finishes and leave all services and the concrete and steel structure bare, obtaining a flexible raw container where they could insert pieces of furniture or create activity spaces that can be modified as needed.

These furnishings plug into the modified exposed services and are made of maple veneer plywood and floating floor, as used for all other surfaces in the building, making them cheap and easy to install or modify.

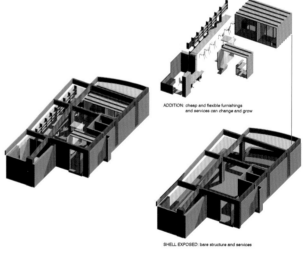

ADDITION: cheap and flexible furnishings
and services can change and grow

SHELL EXPOSED: bare structure and services

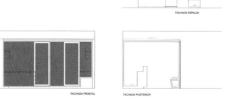

FACHADA ESPALDA

CORTE ASIENTO

FACHADA FRONTAL

FACHADA POSTERIOR

FACHADA FRONTAL

PARTIAL SECTIONS furnishings

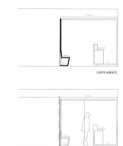

0   1   2   5m

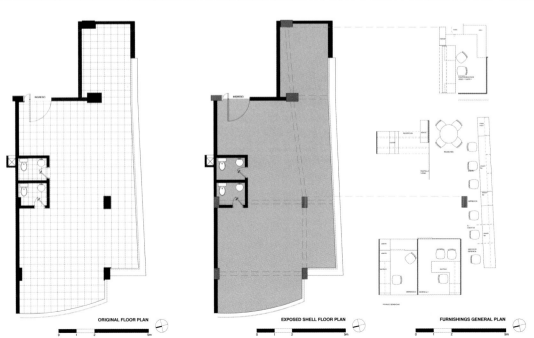

ORIGINAL FLOOR PLAN

EXPOSED SHELL FLOOR PLAN

FURNISHINGS GENERAL PLAN

GENERAL PLAN

Design | Dom Arquitectura
Client | Dom Arquitectura
Photography | Jordi Anguera
Area | 50 sqm
Location | Barcelona, Spain

Dom Studio

The place previously used as a store was completely isolated from the outside. The first action the architects undertook was to open the interior space, both the street and the garden outside, so they designed a completely open, unstudded iron structure with continuous glass that provides natural light throughout the space. All the iron is dark graphite gray painted, the same color as the interior furnishings. The glass surface is placed inside a dark green screen to control the space's privacy.

The inner wall of the room is very irregular. With the goal of unifying all these folds the architects propose some horizontal lines that run through the wall, painted with the same gray as the continuous pavement. This allowed them to provide the wall of a plot in a gradient, continuously and gradually breaking upward toward the roof.

They designed the lamp that runs around the room, from some sections of iron flowing freely through space with convergent and divergent lines, covered with several sheets of folded parchment paper, as if they were the same studio plan. The result is an enlightened paper path through the roof.

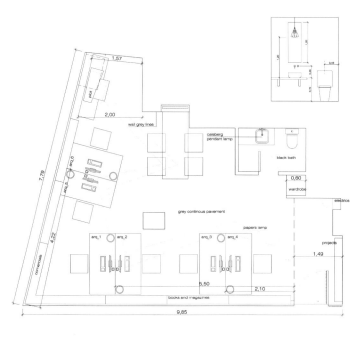

Design | Studio BA
Client | Autodesk
Photography | Ilan Nachum
Area | 500 sqm
Location | Tel Aviv, Israel

Autodesk office – Israel R&D center

The office area is about 500 square meters and located right beside the Tel Aviv harbour; the Israeli R&D center is the AutoCAD WS developers. It contains a mini stand, video game space, relaxation space, dining area, meeting rooms and private / common workspaces.

The 3d multi-material object is made out of steel, glass, wood and fabric. It enables movement around, within and on top of it. The space offers a place to work and take a break. It includes a meeting room, video games lounge, mini stand for lectures / gatherings and a relaxation roof top space, which enables a view of the entire office.

The dining table made from 6mm bent steel was designed as a dual function object. It enables a standard height seating as well as a bar height seating. Its size and position allows the dining space to blend in as an inseparable part of the office.

An open space terrace platform enables a view towards the office and main window while working. It emphasizes its three-dimensionality, by being an object with diverse angles and heights that allows the employees to move through and around it.

470cm

545cm

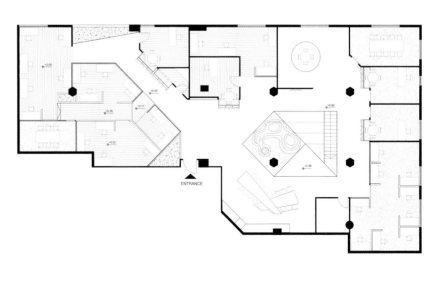

Design | Rios Clementi Hale Studios
Client | Rios Clementi Hale Studios
Photography | Tom Bonner
Area | 17,000 sqft
Location | Los Angeles, US

Larchmont Office

Rios Clementi Hale Studios – Los Angeles-based multi-disciplinary architecture, interiors, landscape architecture, planning, graphic, and product design firm – purchased an existing mini-mall to build on its talent as a retailer / wholesaler, and to expand its office space to accommodate the firm's staff. Renovation of the former mini-mall included replacing the exterior walls with a near floor-to-ceiling window wall system, creating porches of glass and aluminum panels – inspired by the Gamble House sleeping porches – around the second floor studio space, and leveling off the roof surrounding the existing skylights, to upgrade and streamline the space to fit the building into the sophisticated city streetscape.

FIRST FLOOR PLAN

APRIL 11, 2008

SECOND FLOOR PLAN

APRIL 11, 2008

Design | CUBE architecten
Client | Ruigrok | Netpanel
Photography | Roel van Lanen
Area | 525 sqm
Location | Amsterdam, the Netherlands

SILODAM

The main spatial intervention was the invention of the "research-BOX". This holds the extra meeting-room, interview-room and waiting area. Like a big crate of what seems to be huge pieces of plywood, glass and steel, it sits between the big concrete columns right next to the entrance. Some other, more informal places to sit are on the extra floor that hangs between other columns. Here people can get together and discuss projects under the concrete silos that hang from the ceiling. Through the whole office the silos are now used as lighting.

To make the place work like an office, CUBE architecten introduced color and wood to bring just enough warmth to the silo. The Ruigrok | Netpanel colors purple and dark red were used for some furniture and other accents and wood of the before mentioned research-BOX, the desks and tables. Next to the old industrial icons and signs that were left on the concrete silos, several new icons in the same purple color were introduced to show where different functions are located. Art work not only brought more color to the workplace but was also used to get the acoustics of the office to a comfortable level. Because of all the concrete and other hard surfaces, the introduction of softer surfaces was necessary.

1. Lunchruimte
2. Keuken
3. Toiletten
4. Archief en serverhok
5. Werkvloer
6. Wachtruimte
7. Onderzoeksruimte
8. Meekijkruimte
9. Entree
10. Garderobe
11. Stille werkplekken
12. Bibliotheek
13. Vergaderruimte

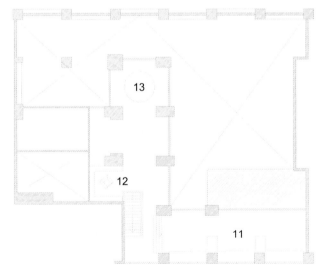

Design | Albert France-Lanord Architects
Client | Bahnhof AB
Photography | Åke E:son Lindman
Area | 1,200 sqm
Location | Stockholm, Sweden

Pionen – White mountain

The project takes place in a former 1,200 square-meter anti-atomic shelter in an amazing location 30 meters down under the granite rocks of the Vita Berg Park in Stockholm. The client is an internet provider and the rock shelter hosts server halls and offices. The starting point of the project was to consider the rock as a living organism. The humans try to acclimate themselves to this foreign world and bring the "best" elements from earth: light, plants, water and technology. The architects created strong contrasts between rooms where the rock dominates and where human

beings are strangers and rooms where the human beings took over totally.

The choice of lighting has been very challenging. The architects tried to bring as much variation as possible. Otherwise it is very easy to lose the feeling of time in an enclosed space.

The references come straight from science fiction films, mostly 'Silent Running' and Bond films with Ken Adams set design.

One can describe the process in six different phases: planning, destruction

of the former office and blowing up the rock to create extra space, reinforcing the cave, technical and electrical installations, glass and steel work, paint and furnishing.

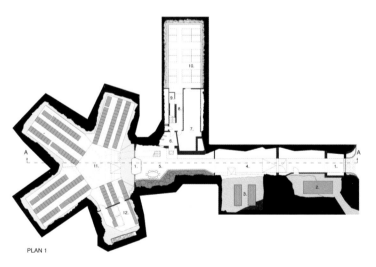

PLAN 1

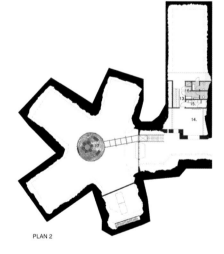

PLAN 2

1. Sluss
2. Kyltorn
3. Dieselutrymme
4. Tunnel
5. Växthus
6. Vestibul
7. Kylsystem och elcentral
8. Korridor
9. Lager
10. Kontor
11. Serverhall
12. Ställverksrum

13. Entré
14. Relaxrum
15. Kök
16. Toaletter och dusch
17. Konferens

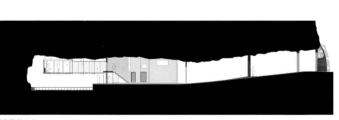

SEKTION A-A

Design | Caterina Tiazzoldi
Client | Toolbox
Photography | Sebastiano Pellion di Persano, Heléné Cany
Area | 1,200 sqm
Location | Torino, Italy

Toolbox, Torino Office Lab & Co-working

The concept of the project has driven every design choice. The walls of the entrance have been achieved with 500 variations of one single white box. The overall design was obtained with parametric software generating endless configurations from a single digital model. Similarly, conditioning grids have been obtained from a single parametric model that recalculates the size and position of the holes based on the exchange of air required in each environment.

The same principle was also applied in the management of space oriented towards sustainable flexibility, which is not based on the transformation of physical space but on a variety of uses obtained through the use of a few combined functions (collaborative working space, meeting rooms, kitchen, patio, parking). It is a flexible structure permitting an almost limitless number of scenarios. An automated system for centralised control of lighting, access, and services (printers, telephones) allows each user to have a profile designed according to their needs. The management of the space is therefore related to an automated system that allows or denies the use of certain functions in accordance with users' profiles. In this way the automated system allows them to reduce direct friction between people with regard to the modality of use of the space. Automation has become a tool of socialization in a space in which interaction between users is very strong.

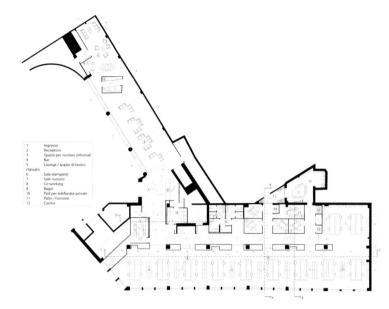

1	Ingresso
2	Reception
3	Spazio per riunioni informali
4	Bar
5	Lounge / spazio di lavoro rilassato
6	Sala stampanti
7	Sale riunioni
8	Co-working
9	Bagni
10	Pod per telefonate private
11	Patio / Fumoire
12	Cucina

1. meeting room
2. elevators
3. type 1 cork meeting room box
4. shinny red meeting room box
5. type 2 cork meeting room box
6. pod internally painted with shinny white enamel
7. glass partition
8. filter volume
9. conditioning grid
10. hangers
11. personal lockers
12. extruded polystyrene parametric cubes

Section C'C

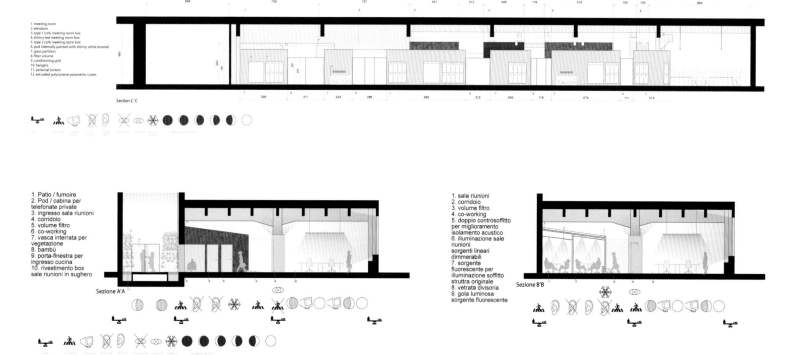

1. Patio / fumoire
2. Pod / cabina per telefonate private
3. ingresso sala riunioni
4. corridoio
5. volume filtro
6. co-working
7. vasca interrata per vegetazione
8. bambù
9. porta-finestra per ingresso cucina
10. rivestimento box sale riunioni in sughero

Sezione A'A

1. sala riunioni
2. corridoio
3. volume filtro
4. co-working
5. doppio controsoffitto per miglioramento isolamento acustico
6. illuminazione sale riunioni
sorgenti lineari dimmerabili
7. sorgente fluorescente per illuminazione soffitto struttura originale
8. vetrata divisoria
9. gola luminosa sorgente fluorescente

Sezione B'B

Design | Sergey Makhno,
Butenko Vasiliy
Client | ---
Photography | ---
Area | 126 sqm
Location | Kyiv, Ukraine

Ukraine design factory, "azure"

The office owner wanted the space to reflect the main characteristics of his company producing design accessories. So the office interior communicates with both its employees and clients through an interesting design concept. Walls have two coverings: the first one is made with Corian and the second is wooden. Wooden undercover can be seen in those places where the top material disperses baring to the bottom layers. At the same time, wood and concrete as undercover materials decorate toilet walls. This modern office space consists of the meeting space, presentation area, workspace, terrace and storage. In its open space, indirect lighting and bright colors make this work space imaginative and exciting, providing inspiration to its inhabitants.

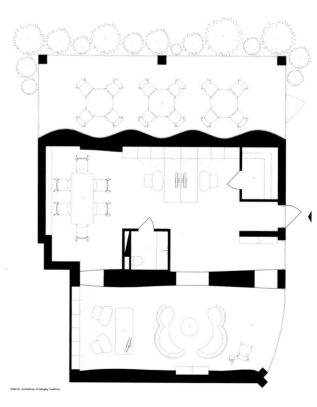

floor plan
1. managers
2. meeting zone
3. designers
4. relax zone
5. products zone
6. wardrobe
7. toilet room
8. terrace

interior workshop of sergey makhno

Design | Because We Can, Inc
Client | Three Rings Design
Photography | Jillian Northrup
Area | 3,500 sqm
Location | San Francisco, US

Three Rings Design Office

The Three Rings Office is homage to Jules Verne's "Nautilus". The office is fun and vibrant for this creative company, complete with room partitions that resemble portholes to the ocean, levers and control panels on the walls, a "tentacle attack" game room, and even a secret room, accessible only through a door built into a bookcase. The company's high employee retention proves the success of this space. The architects asked if some of the artists would like to contribute when they began the designs.

Many of the artists designed the graphics for their own desk, giving the designers Illustrator or Flash files that they integrated into CAM software and turned into furniture.

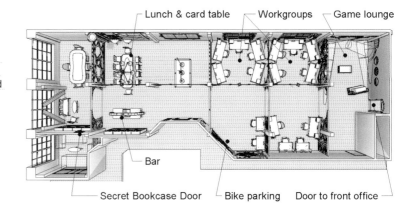

Lunch & card table — Workgroups — Game lounge
Bar
Secret Bookcase Door — Bike parking — Door to front office

Design | Electric Dreams
Client | Fabric Retail Glbl
Photography | Joel Degermark
Area | 1,500 sqm
Location | Gothenburg, Sweden

Fabricville

The inspiration behind this design was the idea that a busy company headquarters is very much like a little village. The aesthetic is very much inspired by traditional Swedish wooden cottages.

The office was originally divided into several offices with different tenants; then it was all thrown together to form the 3-floor, 1500 sqm Fabricville office. The space bore traces of several different, conflicting renovation schemes: some from the 80s, some from the late 90s. The space had endless dull corridors with a mishmash of window and door types, and lots of different ceiling heights.

The Fabricville concept came about as a way to turn all the space's shortcomings into an advantage. The three-floor office was to house 150 employees of Fabric Retail, Weekday and Monki: an interesting mix of fashion designers, buyers, construction managers, and PR people. Their wish was to bring it all together in one visual identity and to house a family of fashion brands, each with its own unique personality.

The long narrow corridors became a busy village street, with workshop buildings for the clothes designers, office buildings for the marketing people, and brightly colored cottages for conference rooms. The main street is lined with laser-cut MDF hedges on each side. The canteen is the green park in the middle. Each floor has a different color scheme to match the identity of the brand situated there.

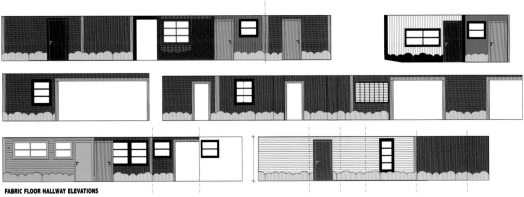

FABRIC FLOOR HALLWAY ELEVATIONS

MONKI FLOOR HALLWAY ELEVATIONS

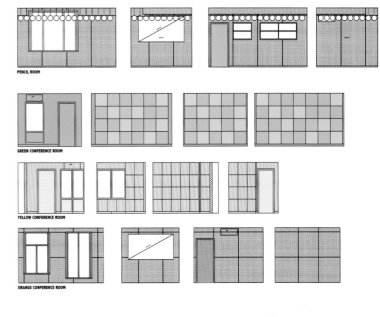

PENCIL ROOM

GREEN CONFERENCE ROOM

YELLOW CONFERENCE ROOM

ORANGE CONFERENCE ROOM

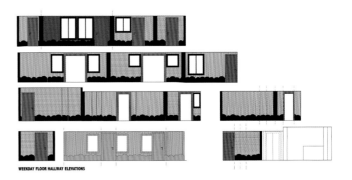

WEEKDAY FLOOR HALLWAY ELEVATIONS

Design | PS Arkitektur
Client | Skype
Photography | Jason Strong
Area | 1,680 sqm
Location | Stockholm, Sweden

Skype office

The project consists of audio and video studios, offices and social areas for 100 employees. The core thought of the Skype software application has generated the design concept for the interior of the new office. The core thought is that Skype is a useful and playful tool that allows chats, voice and video calls all over the Internet. From this idea the spaces between the several abstracted interconnected nodes are extruded from the idea of the interconnected world. The scheme of this abstraction replicates itself in the flooring and in the design of the fixed interior. The idea of the loose bubbly furniture has evolved from the Skype logos. The Skype cloud known as the Skype logo has been literally reinterpreted as a cloud-shaped lighting fixture, shining throughout the chill out space. The lighting fixture, truly one of its kind, is created by a cluster of lit up translucent globes of various sizes.

Created within a former brewery, a major effort has been made in order to accomplish high-end acoustics in the venue, efforts such as installing and designing soft wall absorbers. These efforts have been necessary for an office that predominately works with audio and video development. This focus on audio and video development is visible in the interior and expressed in the unique wallpapers with prints of cables, earphones and other devices linked to the audio-video technique.

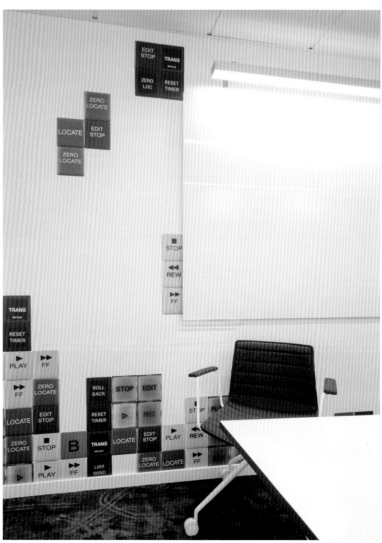

Design | Ippolito Fleitz Group
Client | Ippolito Fleitz Group GmbH
Photography | Zooey Braun
Area | 480 sqm
Location | Stuttgart, Germany

Studio Ippolito Fleitz Group

The studio found new premises in a former factory for control technology in the west of Stuttgart. The five-storey Gründerzeit building was originally built at the turn of the last century to house an industrial laundry. Largely reconstructed after the war due to heavy bombing damage, the first floor of the building retains something of the building's original character as a production facility. The four-metre high ceiling is supported by cast-iron pillars, a feature rarely found in Stuttgart, giving the space a nostalgic feel. With

a floor area of almost 500m², the studio provides the necessary space for free, creative thinking. Inspired by the building's original design of individual rooms assembled around a stairwell, each area was given its own separate identity, the sum of which tells a coherent story.

Two long work desks cultivate a creative and communicative atmosphere. Shelving and furniture are executed in white or dark wood. Contrasting accents of color are set by textile bands

above the workplaces that serve as light switches, and the areas of green plants. In addition to two conference rooms, cheerful communication islands are available for discussions. The studio with spacious kitchen and oversized mirror is a place of both inspiration and relaxation.

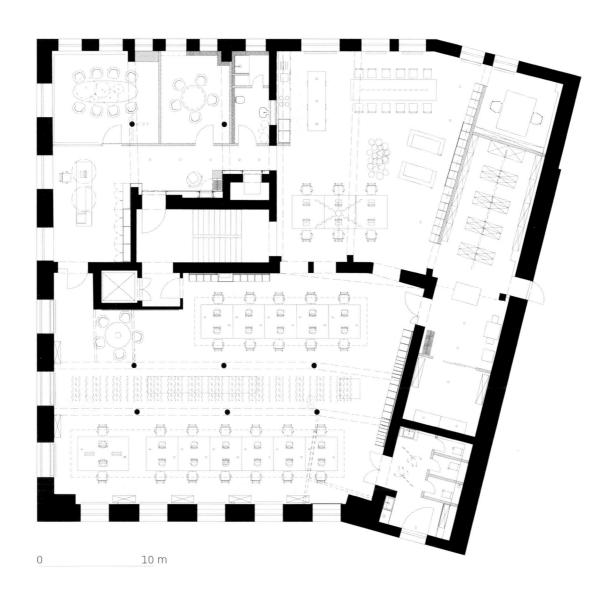

0 ⟨──────⟩ 10 m

Design | PS Arkitektur
Client | Dynabyte
Photography | Erika Janunger
Area | 1,400 sqm
Location | Stockholm, Sweden

Dynabyte office

The interior signals playfulness and the enjoyment of being in your own place. It also reflects the genuinely cheerful and friendly spirit the company radiates.

To make the company's expertise in computer programming visible, the color scheme was picked up from the first few html-colors available at the birth of Internet. The wallpapers in the conference rooms are all custom-made ASCII-artworks and the rooms themselves are designed in themes of sea, forest and city.

Workstations have to be truly flexible as people constantly change project teams and as a result of that, cords and electronics are all over the place. Instead of trying to hide and complicate this problem that cannot be hidden or solved, the cords are made part of the color concept and create a colorful and fun element.

The wallpapers and door coverings are custom-made photographs of reality – a kind of meta-concept where nothing is what it seems to be, quite like the digital world itself where nothing is "for real" but exists because it depicts the real world. Kitchen tiles, doors and even objects on the shelves have all put on their finest masquerade costumes to take part in the playful concept.

Design | Lehrer Architects
Client | Lehrer Architects
Photography | Benny Chan / Fotoworks
Area | 5,400 sqft
Location | Los Angeles, US

Lehrer Architects LA

Lehrer Architects met the challenge by turning the building into a working space of light, air, and transparency. The project included succinct interventions, such as blowing out the southern wall, creating 4x8 work surfaces of white-painted solid core doors, finishing floors with epoxy, installing off-the-shelf storage systems, painting a dramatic red line along the floor to resolve the trapezoidal shape of the space, and creating a strategic landscape design. The total cost of $20 per square foot encompasses the mechanical / electrical / data / telephone infrastructure, garden, and build-out of all work surfaces.

Although the office would specifically house architects, the architects designed a multipurpose working space that simply and clearly honors the rudiments of work: vast work surfaces, massive natural light, seamless connections to the landscape and fresh air, generous storage, and clearly individuated workstations that add up to a coherent, palpable group.

The visitor is immediately drawn into the architecture – which is about the beauty of making architecture. The space succeeds as an open, collaborative working lab for creative design.

In addition to the creation of meaningful architecture, the office is host to community events, drawing classes, and municipal design reviews. The innovative design of this adaptive-reuse project has garnered a long list of accolades and awards.

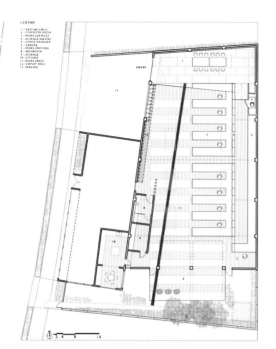

LEGEND
1 - MEETING SPACE
2 - COMPUTER ROOM
3 - WORK SURFACES
4 - STORAGE SHELVES
5 - OFFICE MANAGER
6 - GARDEN
7 - WORK STATIONS
8 - STORAGE
9 - STORAGE
10 - KITCHEN
11 - WORK SPACE
12 - DISPLAY WALL
13 - PARKING

Design | SELGASCANO
Client | SELGASCANO
Photography | Iwan Baan, Roland Halbe
Area | 70 sqm
Location | Madrid, Spain

STUDIO SELGASCANO

What is being sought in this studio is quite simple: working under the trees. To achieve this, the architects needed a roof that was as transparent as possible. Also, they need to isolate the desk zone from direct sunlight.

The transparent northern part is covered with a bent sheet of 20mm colourless plexiglass on the north side. The southern side, where the desks are located, has to be closed much more, but not completely, so there is a double sheet of fibreglass and polyester in its natural colour on the southern side, with translucent insulation in the middle. All three form a 110mm thick sandwich.

In the former case, the outward view is clear and transparent. The views in the latter case are translucent and somewhat marred by the cantilevered metal structure left inside the sandwich, with the shadow of the trees projecting onto it gently.

This simplicity will mature later on into an extremely complex structure. The architects mean to say complex in the sense that it was impossible to convince a company to get involved in such a small building from start to finish, with components straight from the catalogue, but which were not for catalogue-style assembly, forcing them to contract the work out under what is known as

"the administration" procedure, with a timetable that more or less fit into when the construction companies were available.

Everything placed below ground level is in concrete with wood framework – wooden planks that are also used for paving, firmly bolted and painted in two colours with two components with an epoxy base.

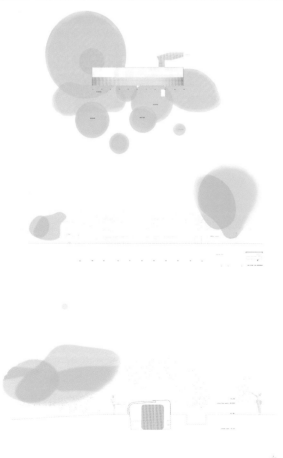

Design | elisavalero
Client | Elisa Valero Ramos
Photography | Fernando Alda
Area | 198.60 sqm
Location | Granada, Spain

Elisa Valero Ramos office

The program is as exceptional as the tiny lot on Belén Street. It is adapted to stack work areas and a living space for a single person without renouncing quality and spatial wealth. And it does so with very straightforward means, such as the manipulation of natural light, varying heights indoors to compensate for the narrowness of the rooms, and of course, an absolute minimum of compartmentalization. Thus, the stairs and service areas are at the end, leaving the central spaces free.

Precision calls for solving problems by minimizing them, that is, with the smallest possible outlay to meet technical and functional requirements. These considerations underlie the project, which is conceived as a section of the wall that historically separated the city from outlying farmland. And that is how the project was approached: a wall pierced with narrow, regular openings and a single opening on the upper part. Like a traditional Granada house, it is closed to the street but open to the sky and garden.

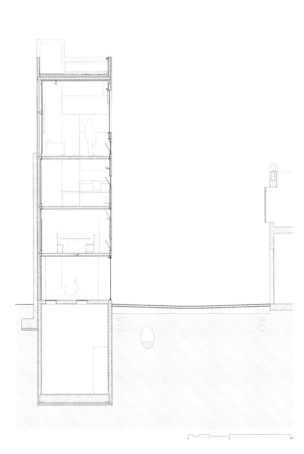

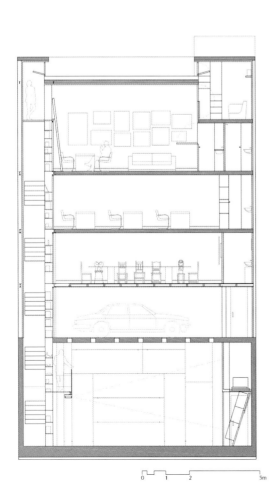

0   1   2   5m

Design | Jackie-B
Client | Cubion a/s
Photography | Jacob Nielsen
Area | 178 sqm
Location | Copenhagen, Denmark

Cubion Office Copenhagen

Located in the heart of Copenhagen the consultant company Cubion a/s now occupies the lower floor in a protected house dated back from 1793 The house is right out to one of the major pedestrian streets in the oldest par of Copenhagen.

Jackie-B turned the office into three different rooms for exchange of knowledge and conversation with simplicity in color and design. The main office supports and stimulates the exchange of knowledge. The office space is suited for eight employees divided into two groups of juicy green tables. The Office is lid up by two suspended lamps also designed for the room by Jackie-B. The office walls are decorated with synthetic grass islands that allow the possibility to lean on and help to secure a dreamy and calm atmosphere. A brainstorm grid on the glass wall is used as entrench and whiteboard which secures privacy from the office surroundings.

The kitchen is designed as a social meeting room with a bright yellow table that centers the room. A forest Photostat leads to the back office where a graphic display of a childhood house stands as a shining white memory with small lamps flowers. The sofa house offers space for deep thoughts and loose conversations. The back office also contains external work space so employees can retrieve and work away from the main office.

The office is designed to support and stimulate an environment that gives the employees and customers a new experience of what an office can be.

Design | mode:lina architektura & consulting
Client | mode:lina
Photography | Marcin Dondajewski
Area | 55.9 sqm
Location | Poznan, Poland

OSB Office

Faithful to the idea of using cheap materials without a cheap appearance, designers used lacquered OSB boards for the flooring and furniture. Desks, also made of OSB, are covered with artificial leather to make sketching and drawing more comfortable. Luminaries are produced out of standard profiles used for gypsum-cardboard wall systems. Furniture in the OSB office creates an intimate atmosphere and hides all the cabling and recycling bins.

Design | upsetters architects
Client | WOW
Photography | Yusuke Wakabayashi
Area | 188 sqm
Location | Sendai, Japan

WOW Sendai

The office is slender and located in the office building in front of Sendai Station. It also commands a panoramic view of the city and is comparatively large for the number of employees.

The working space is loosely divided into four sections according to the professions with no clear boundary. However, it is attempted that all the personal spaces are set apart enough so that better concentration will be possible, but without a feeling of isolation.

Cut timbers are piled up by the windows, with which people can flexibly compose what they want. They are supposed to be used as a bench, a desk and so on. The communication in the "free" space would not be such a formal meeting but a beneficial chat about current projects and situations.

The reason the designers just piled up cut timber instead of complete furniture is that the workers can participate in the spatial design even during their use of the space. Moreover, the redundancy

and incompleteness challenges their thought process.

The blank space at the entrance is expected to be used for examination of their installation work. It is, therefore, covered with artificial turf so that people can sit on the floor.

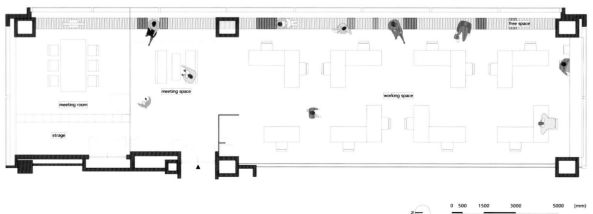

meeting room

strage

meeting space

working space

free space

0 500 1500 3000 5000 (mm)

Design | Ippolito Fleitz Group
Client | Bruce B. GmbH
Photography | Zooey Braun
Area | 480 sqm
Location | Stuttgart, Germany

Bruce B. / Emmy B. Design agency

The aim in designing a suitable interior for the agency was to faithfully translate what epitomises its work into architecture. Objects and design elements initially appear to be in diametric opposition, yet strike a harmonious balance throughout.

Antitheses attract the visitor's attention from the very first moment of entering the agency, beginning with the shape of the reception desk. It is crafted in exposed concrete, which displays an added materiality in the form of the visible structure of the wooden plank mould. The concrete form is topped by a white, lacquered surface. Antithetical details are also present in the adjoining conference rooms – usually the second point of call for the agency's clients. The walls of the smaller conference room are panelled with maritime pine boards. Narrow yellow grooves refine their appearance, which would normally invoke simple packing crates, transforming them into attractive room panelling. The large conference room next door is dominated by a long conference table with randomly spaced table legs breaking up the sober impression it would otherwise have made. Directing your gaze towards the ceiling of the reception area and conference rooms allows you to take in another unusual detail: Stucco elements have been added to the ceiling joists, recalling the coziness of an old apartment building in the very midst of this industrial landscape.

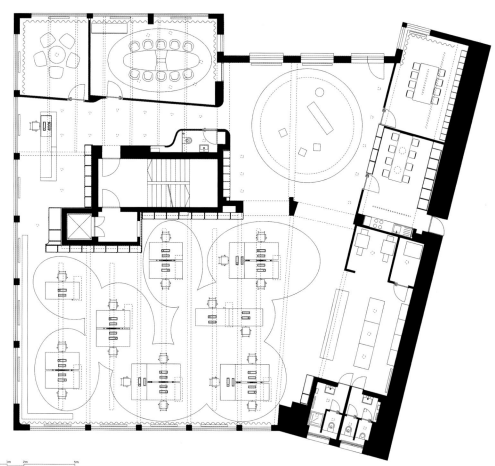

Design | Maurice Mentjens Design
Client | PostPanic
Photography | Arjen Schmitz
Area | ---
Location | Amsterdam, the Netherlands

PostPanic

Designer Maurice Mentjens has fitted up PostPanic's Amsterdam studio as a professional playground that emphasizes the company's creative, headstrong attitude.

In the design Mentjens took the existing concrete structure, and more specifically the large concrete columns, as his point of departure. The distance between the columns defines the dimensions of the subsequent areas. The width of production room, meeting room and staff room measures the span between two columns; the studio up on the mezzanine measures twice this size.

By introducing the mezzanine, Mentjens creates the required floor space without compromising the studio's open feel. Because the low floor height doesn't allow a lowered ceiling, pipes stay on display. Combined with the large concrete columns, the smooth concrete floors, the lack of thresholds and the fluorescent tubes on the ceiling, this emphasizes the slightly raw, industrial feel the interior has to it.

In accordance to the briefing, every single department has its own distinctive atmosphere. Mentjens' conceptual approach guarantees that the different atmospheres come together as one world – the different areas are segregated, not isolated, and offer the possibility to stay in touch with each other; construction materials are used consistently. The informal feel of the design has emphasized PostPanic's philosophy. This dynamic, inviting environment surely offers PostPanic all the required room to play.

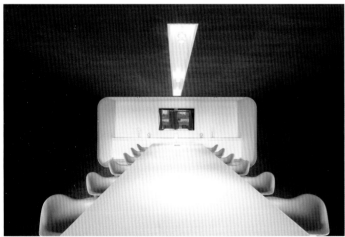

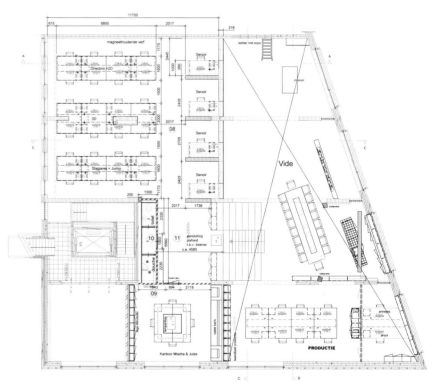

Design | HASSELL
Client | PTT Exploration and Production
Public Company Limited
Photography | Owen Raggett
Area | 45,000 sqm
Location | Bangkok, Thailand

PTTEP Headquarters

HASSELL created an open plan workplace for PTTEP, configured around new internal stairways that provide a physical and visual link between all 18 levels of the 45,000 square-meter tenancy.

Breakout and hub spaces are situated close to stair landings, encouraging staff interaction and promoting visual connection between departments. Utility rooms, located around the central core, ensure work space areas are positioned with close proximity to natural light. This open plan approach is a significant change for PTTEP and

has strengthened the culture of the company.

The interior color scheme, inspired by the luminous gas flame associated with oil exploration and production, created a unique identity across the floors. This "Color of Flame" concept was the key component linking vertical spaces, as the stair and floor group color coding changed from green, through blue, light blue, yellow and red as it rose up the building. At night this element is a highly visible external statement.

The introduction of a dedicated client floor, complete with meeting rooms

and extensive audiovisual facilities, and a separate executive suite accommodating all management facilities, enabled PTTEP to maximize the general workplace facilities on other floors.

Two landscaped external roof decks provide additional space for staff recreation and other corporate activities. Established trees and vertical wall climbers create a lush and green environment to complement the building's glazed truss parapet.

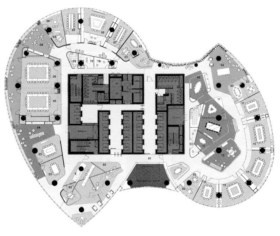

Level 18
scale 1:250

01 water feature
02 reception and waiting area
03 informal meeting rooms
04 breakout area
05 training room
06 casual meeting room
07 media response room
08 emergency room
09 kitchen
10 security - internal jogging room
11 meeting rooms
12 executive lounge

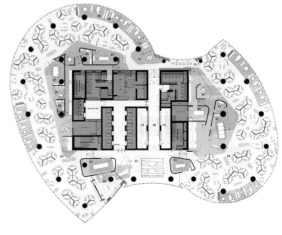

Level 25
scale 1:250

00 lift core (gallery space)
01 waiting area
02 small breakout space
03 meeting room
04 general workspace
05 utility
06 brainstorm room
07 core meeting room
08 no offices
09 manager offices
10 quiet room
11 discussion zones
12 touchdown area
13 storage (compactus)

Design | HASSELL
Client | Total Access Communication
Photography | Pirak Anurakyawachon
Area | 62,000 sqm
Location | Bangkok, Thailand

dtac House

HASSELL designed the new dtac workplace across 20 floors in Chumchuri Square. To support dtac's varied promotional activities as one of Thailand's leading telecommunication providers, an extensive three-level open front-of-house atrium is linked by a new internal feature stairway. This provided a highly adaptable space, able to host a wide variety of client and staff events.

Spaces are defined as volumes rather than by function, and the rich and varied use of local timbers for flooring, screening and ceiling battens provides direction and framework across this activity-based workplace.

The team-based environments encourage dtac staff to be mobile and creative in their choice of work space; whether at their work station, in one of the varied meeting lounges or on the open terrace overlooking Bangkok's skyline. Open workspaces are supplemented with indoor plants, and the incorporation of a dedicated relaxation and fitness floor further enhances staff happiness and promotes a healthy work environment.

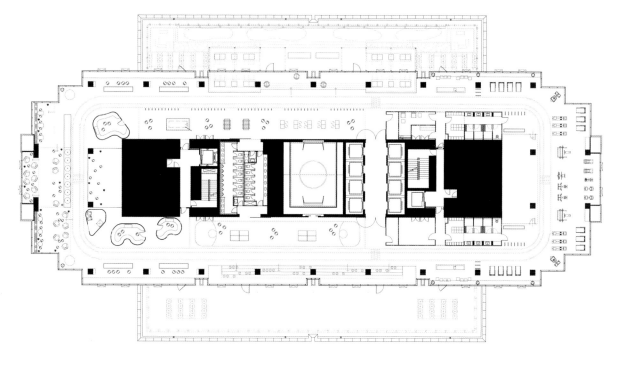

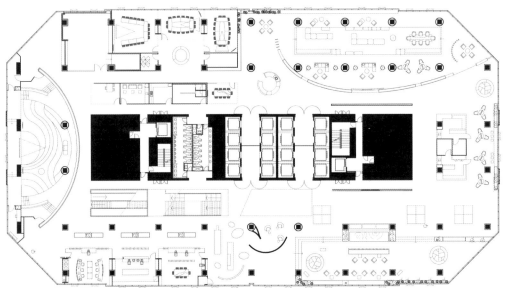

Design | SPACE, Juan Carlos Baumgartner, Fabiola Troyo del Valle
Client | Prodigy MSN
Photography | Paul Czitrom
Area | 890 sqm
Location | Mexico City, Mexico

Prodigy MSN

The openness and translucency are evident in the whole project. The layout incorporates as much daylight as possible. Most of the glass façade is free, but there are a few spots in which some meeting rooms and private offices are next to the façade. Those spaces are closed with glass to allow the openness and brightness they were looking for. In addition, the workstations are low and they have translucent boards.

Finally, in the heart of the project there was built a long row of private offices, conceptualized as a glass box. Some graphic patterns made of vinyl were designed to make these spaces more private but also open, which is in line with the style of Prodigy MSN.

The reception space is a node where employees, clients and visitors enter. Directly inside, there is a coffee bar to make the process of entering more hospitable. There is no board separating this entryway from the work space, and most of the meeting rooms are located in this node.

The offices have a variety of casual meeting rooms located in strategic points to allow communication among employees, and some of them have additional functions.

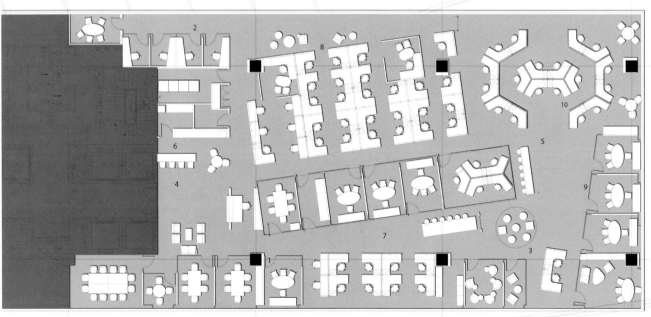

1. PRIVATE OFFICE
2. PHONE BOOTH
3. CASUAL COLLITION
4. RECEPTION / WAITING AREA
5. NEWS ROOM
6. CAFETERIA
7. RECYCLING AREA
8. OPEN AREA
9. MEETING ROOM
10. EXECUTIVE PRODUCER

Design I SPACE, Juan Carlos Baumgartner, Jimena Fernández Navarra
Client I Google
Photography I Willem Schalkwijk
Area I 850 sqm
Location I Mexico City, Mexico

Google

The design concept of Google's offices is really simple: the experience of browsing the web.

Entering the reception area, one finds this really white space, with a bright colored back wall and white flooring, walls and ceilings as a never ending wrapping environment that represents the first encounter which the web.

Once inside, color is obvious, with different layers that make people discover new things as they walk by. The design as a whole maintains that what happens on the ceiling has a direct repercussion on the floor and walls.

An open workspace creates productivity and concentration in a really busy environment. A central circular meeting room represents the heart of the design, around which the other meeting rooms and private offices orbit. A yellow box is a Zen-like space that serves as the transition area into the informal workspace.

Phone booths, ping pong tables, huddle lounges, a shower and the cafeteria create the image of a plaza inside the office, where most of the work is done in different dynamics.

Every door in this office is a different color, giving each one a sense of individuality.

Food and catering is really important for the company to give to their employees, so the kitchen was an important part in the design. It turned out to be an industrial space with technologically advanced fixtures.

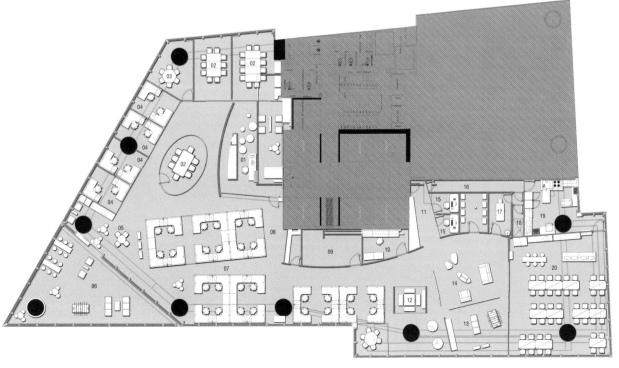

01 Reception
02 Meeting room
03 Huddle
04 Shared office
05 Micro Kitchen
06 Terrace
07 Open area
08 Storage
09 Server room
10 IT storage
11 MKT storage
12 Tech stop
13 Gaming area
14 Informal lounge
15 Phone booth
16 Service hallway
17 Massage room
18 Shower
19 Kitchen
20 Coffe area

Design | SPACE, Juan Carlos
Baumgartner, Fabiola Troyo del Valle
Client | Alsea
Photography | ---
Area | 6,000 sqm
Location | Mexico

Alsea

The challenge of the project was to design a space that housed Alsea's new branch of around 6,000m².

The resulting concept was the idea of generating "Alsea city", a space with an urban touch that operated on the basis of neighborhoods – each neighborhood bringing together a brand, and each of these spaces having a "neighborhood center". The neighborhood centers became the ideal pretexts to generate identity for each group through informal meeting areas or what the architects call "casual collisions".

The architectural layout arises from the idea of maximizing natural light and distributing the private offices perpendicular to the façades, thus liberating the façades to the highest extent possible.

The number and form of the board meeting areas was defined after an extensive investigation. Some of these areas were resolved with unconventional spaces such as pool tables or informal lounges.

The used space is formed by two architectural stories intercommunicated

by an interconnecting stair and, in the center of these spaces, a mezzanine that works as council room was designed. This council room came into being through a glass box lined with texts that express the company's culture and values.

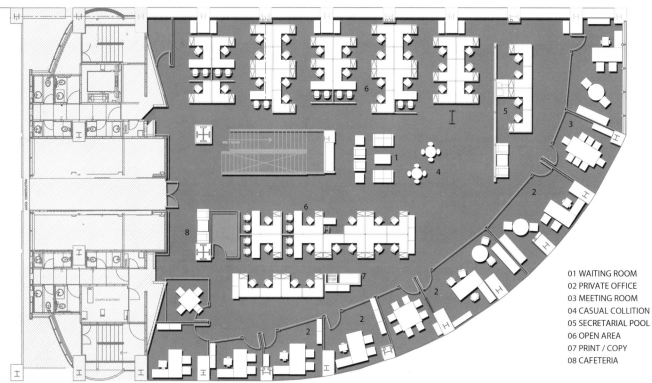

01 WAITING ROOM
02 PRIVATE OFFICE
03 MEETING ROOM
04 CASUAL COLLITION
05 SECRETARIAL POOL
06 OPEN AREA
07 PRINT / COPY
08 CAFETERIA

Design | SPACE, Juan Carlos Baumgartner, Jimena Fernández Navarra
Client | Astra Zeneca
Photography | Alpha Hardin
Area | 6,000 sqm
Location | Mexico City, Mexico

Astra Zeneca

The aim of the project was to maximize natural light and vistas within the premises by placing the built spaces to the sides and using translucent façades to allow light to penetrate the rest of the space, freeing up the longest façade to maximize the availability of natural light.

To make the best use of the floor, all the services were sent to the rear blind part of the building. For the lighting of this space, a lighting fixture was specially designed for the project, creating continuous lines of lighting fixtures with minimum dimensions with a 100% industrial look to the lighting. There are overhead lines at 2.60 intercepting the ceiling where the line is recessed. The space is zoned in accordance with European standard lighting levels and the perception of human beings.

As the building has a very generous height, the aim was to create a more human scale for the front end of the built spaces, with doors and screens of up to 2.80 and from there a light box which serves to emphasize the elevations, while giving the space an industrial feeling.

The use of vinyl bearing the corporate logo throughout the built areas reflects pride in the company and provides a sense of identity that was lacking in the previous location.

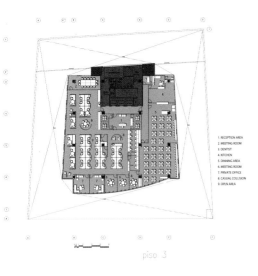

1. RECEPTION AREA
2. MEETING ROOM
3. DENTIST
4. KITCHEN
5. DINNING AREA
6. MEETING ROOM
7. PRIVATE OFFICE
8. CASUAL COLLISION
9. OPEN AREA

piso 3

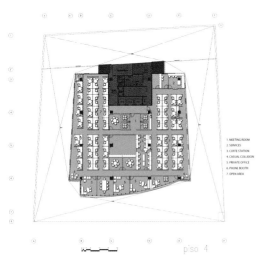

1. MEETING ROOM
2. SERVICES
3. COFFE STATION
4. CASUAL COLLISION
5. PRIVATE OFFICE
6. PHONE BOOTH
7. OPEN AREA

piso 4

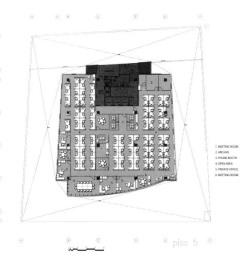

1. MEETING ROOM
2. ARCHIVE
3. PHONE BOOTH
4. OPEN AREA
5. PRIVATE OFFICE
6. MEETING ROOM

piso 5

Design | za bor architects
Client | Forward Media Group
Photography | Peter Zaytsev
Area | 4,200 sqm
Location | Moscow, Russia

Forward Media Group office

Office space was destined to be quite complex – it was a huge loft of 4,200 sqm, significantly elongated and located in the mansard level of a new business center. The situation was made worse by the peculiarity of the publishing house – the need for editorial offices with open spaces as well as commercial and retail departments, separate offices for directors and editors-in-chief with a conference corner, conference halls, an archive with a library, storage rooms, etc. All of these facilities were placed along the corridor going through the whole room. Eventually, open space offices were concentrated on one side, and cabinets were mainly located on the other side of the corridor.

Communication points were supposed to be transparent and not to be overlooked in a homogeneous office. As a result, the elevator lobby with stones, bright reception areas, and meeting rooms was emphasized; a yellow complex construction hides the entrances to the toilets; the archive room was marked by the black floral pattern. The same care was given to the specific build-in furniture designated by za bor architects for visitors. In contrast, operational areas are designed in neutral gray.

Technical wiring placed under a ceiling of the mansard level, as well as rafters and balks have not been hidden, but were painted in black instead, which visually elevates and extends the ceiling.

Architects | COEN! design agency
Client | Besturenraad / BKO, Woerden
Photography | COEN! | Roy van de Meulengraaf
Area | 2,200 sqm
Location | Woerden, the Netherlands

Office Besturenraad | BKO

COEN! created a new working environment and identity layer for the "Besturenraad / BKO". These two organizations are going to cooperate more intensively at a new location and take care of two denominational types of education in the Netherlands: Catholic and Protestant. The aim of this project was to visually connect the shared goals and principles of both organizations.

For the design of this story COEN! used The Book as a metaphor. Apart from the Christian and Catholic values a book also consists of structure, text and image. You see stained glass patterns, metal grids based on the golden section and special text prints with a message. The relation between faith and education is also subtly made clear by DNA patterns and golden "office altars".

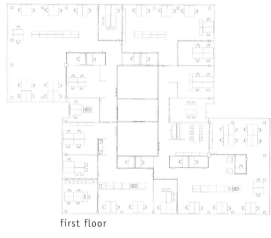

first floor

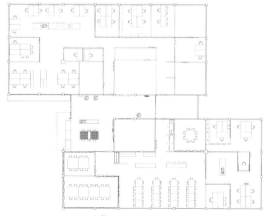

ground floor

Design I architecture3S
Client I HubSpot
Photography I Greg Premru
Photography
Area I 38,000 sqft
Location I Cambridge, MA USA

HubSpot

Hubspot was moving from their bare bones start-up space to a new office space located in a 38,000 square foot series of interconnected mill buildings in Cambridge, Massachusetts.

Inexpensive materials come together in a unique composition that respects the budget, yet yields a spatially rich environment that is not reliant on expensive materials and finishes for its success. Strategically using more expensive materials such as floor to ceiling glazing and offsetting those costs with simple painted drywall, laminate surfaces and inexpensive linear strip fluorescent fixtures backlighting a

cellular plastic panel dropped into an ordinary ceiling grid, creates a signature aesthetic. Introducing the client's branding logo and colors into the design tailors the space.

The misalignment of the floors from mill building to mill building was seized as an opportunity to design in enhanced thresholds that informed the user that they were moving from one building to another. Realized as simple painted drywall tubes, these thresholds establish a sense of place and work to celebrate the circulation through the spaces.

Materials such as translucent curtains and birch stalks are used to soften

the space in juxtaposition to the more minimal and machined surfaces. The curtains provide an enhanced acoustic quality at the lobby that also serves as a break out area for the adjacent multi-purpose room and conference rooms. Birch stalks are used similarly and provide a contrast that is warm, unique and beautiful to walk by or form an edge at impromptu meeting locations outside the space's typical circulation.

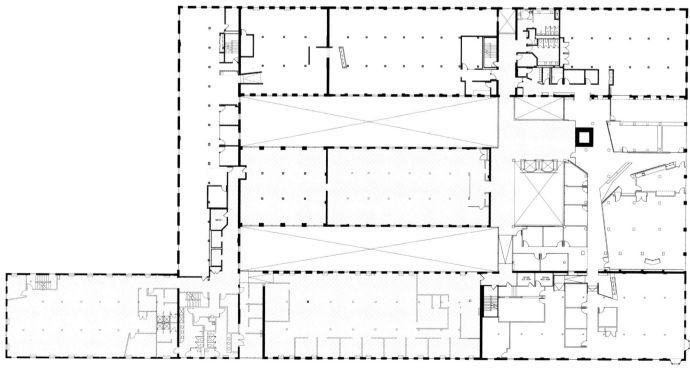

Design | architecture3S
Client | KAYAK.COM
Photography | Greg Premru
Photography
Area | 11,430 sqft
Location | Concord, MA USA

KAYAK.COM

Office designs are comprised of a very simple kit of parts: enclosed offices, open offices, conference rooms, kitchens and utility spaces such as server rooms, etc. The joy is taking those elements and transforming them into the extraordinary. Creating an environment that is unexpected provides an oasis for employees. It tells them that they are special and their company is doing something unique.

The design for the world headquarters of KAYAK.COM purposefully defines private employee spaces from public congregational employee spaces.

The separation assists in providing areas of destination within the overall environment that have purpose and focus. Conference rooms, a café and an informal open area are organized around the entry circulation into the space to make that procession lively and active. A change in lighting, materials and scale establishes a physical and perceptual cue that transitions into the private work area. Typically hidden functions such as the server room are predominantly featured to form an edge to the circulation into the space. Enveloped with the KAYAK.

COM signature orange, glass walls turn the server room into a showpiece. Accompanied by a suspended acoustic panel system, a backlit stretched ceiling and an operable glass wall to the conference room, the materials assist in directing movement through the space and blur the rigid spatial definitions of the program.

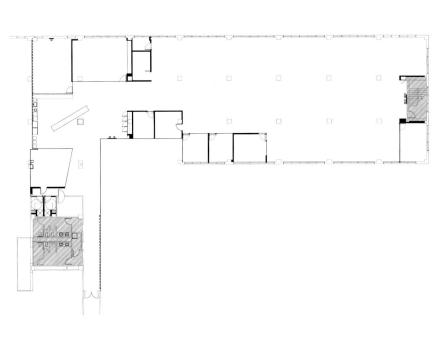

Design | architecture3S
Client | LogMeIn
Photography | Greg Premru
Photography
Area | 14,500 sqft
Location | Woburn, MA USA

LogMeIn

In stark contrast to LogMeIn's existing ordinary workspace, the new environment reaches the same functional and cost effective achievements, but in a completely reinterpreted way. Conceived as embracing forms made out of painted surfaces, café counters, lighting and curtains, these elements work in concert to envelop the space and create an environment that is dynamic, active and engaging. This multi-purpose space stands centrally located about the office plan and is a threshold between the old and new expanded office. Acting as an object in the work space, employees can see it from their work stations; they can circulate around and through it during their work day. The new space also serves as an iconic feature that defines the growth of their business and the excitement of their success, interpreted architecturally.

For functional reasons, the space employs operable curtains and acoustic ceiling tile to assist in sound absorption. This removes any inconvenience to those working in proximity to the room. Inexpensive and functional, these design features assist in sculpting the ceiling plane and vertical surfaces to move people through the space as well as creating pockets of activity. Other inexpensive devices such as painted drywall, vinyl floor tile and linear strip fluorescent fixtures come together to assist in the feeling of movement and dynamism.

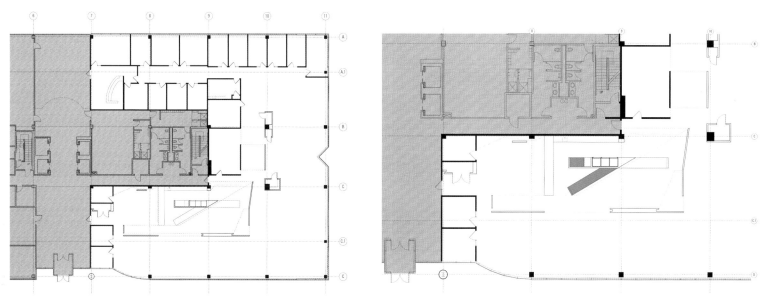

Design | za bor architects
Client | Yandex Company
Photography | Peter Zaytsev
Area | 720 sqm
Location | Yekaterinburg, Russia

Yandex Yekaterinburg office

The Yandex office in Yekaterinburg is the 4th office by za bor architects designed for this company. The office occupies the fifteenth floor of a new business center "Palladium". The building is horseshoe-shaped. The office spaces are concentrated around the center.

Dynamic volumes and expressive furniture is za bor architects' visiting card; they successfully convey the concept of a prompt exponential

"Yandex" development, while wood and cork is chosen as the main surface materials to illustrate the company's humanism. Thin partitions and the wood used in construction are not just aesthetic – they also have a soundproofing function. Low ceilings (3.60m) have been visually made higher in the corridor, and the communications there have been painted a deep black color. Work areas have Ecophon insulated ceilings for better sound absorption.

Internet wiring and electrical cables are contained in the raised floor. The flooring chosen is carpet tile, which allows quick access to the technology and wiring hidden below the floor.

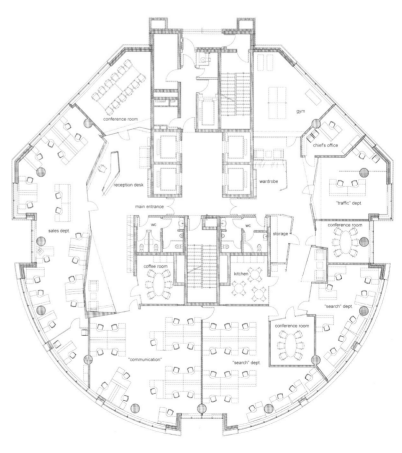

Design | Marcos Samaniego / MAS ARQUITECTURA
Client | MNProgram
Photography | Ana Samaniego
Area | 415.42 sqm
Location | A Coruña, Spain

MNProgram Office

The office, located in A Coruña (Spain), is characterized by high quality materials, views of the Atlantic Ocean, and relaxing spaces, including a living room with plasma TV and sofas and a nice kitchen where people enjoy snacks.

The design focuses on open spaces. Consequently, workspaces have been arranged longitudinally along the large window, in order to take advantage of natural light and provide employees with spectacular views of the Atlantic Ocean. As a result, movement inside is agile and direct.

A quadrilateral space, called "the ring", dominates the central space of the office. Built with wood, "the ring" offers creatives a pure atmosphere to work away from the daily stress.

Other spaces, such as a bathroom with access over a footbridge, or the kitchen equipped with TV, sofa and pantry, contribute to employees' enjoyment. Indeed, natural light from the Atlantic sea makes it easier to spend a day in this office, designed by Marcos Samaniego Reimundez, from Mas Arquitectura.

The project includes high quality materials. Natural wood finishes are combined with satin-finishes in the work space. Grass is a special guest. Remarkably soft grass covers not only the floor but also several walls.

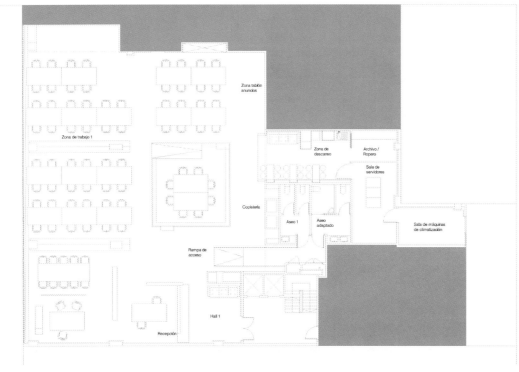

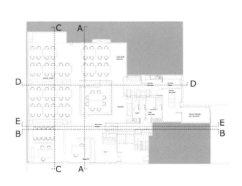

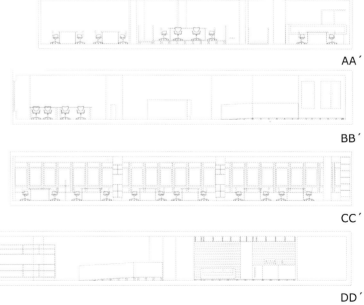

AA´

BB´

CC´

DD´

EE´

Design | MMASA Studio
Client | Konstruplus
Photography | Hector Fernández
Santos-Díez
Area | ---
Location | A Coruña, Spain

Konstruplus Offices

Once the original building was emptied, a series of girders and pillars was discovered. A continuous surrounding was built from this base, as much in the vertical plane as the horizontal one. This sinuous surrounding creates several environments that serve to sequence the privacy of the small office without needing rigid vertical divisions.

To complement these goals for the space, MMASA Studio introduced an illuminated garden that turns into the backbone of the office, contributing the necessary light for the work space with limited dimensions and scant natural lighting.

After having arranged the vertical and horizontal paraments with these statements, the designers considered it important to eliminate any type of zenithal light, canalizing the luminosity across the dry garden that is protected and reinforced by some white strings. The lighting of the tables is completed with lights over each work space.

The colors that they employed combine the corporate image of the company – green and black – with the necessary white color that lends more spaciousness to the feel of the space.

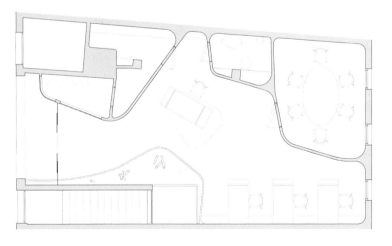

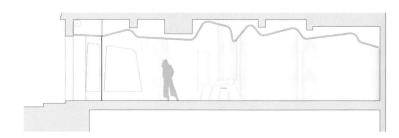

Design | Estudio Mytaki
Client | Tourist Board of Granada
Photography | Fernando Alda, Estudio Mytaki
Area | 160 sqm
Location | Granada, Spain

Tourist Information Office

The Tourist Board of Granada's Provincial Council decided to renew its office's image. Previously, half of the floor space was dedicated to storage and only a minimum was allowed for customer service.

Estudio Mytaki proposed two basic improvements. The first was the clearing up of space in the interior, and the second was the development of this free space into a welcoming environment for tourists, a breathing body with shape and movements formed by furniture.

Stainless steel is a versatile material resistant to daily wear and the ceiling, walls and floor are all formed from the same steel section. Adapting the space and possibilities, the previous brick, marble and patios coexist with contemporary architecture to create a single, dynamic image.

1 Entrance
2 Tourist reception room
3 Attention to disabled people
4 Media room
5 Tourist service
6 Tourist room
7 Office
8 Courtyard
9 Foyer
10 Toilet

office furniture #1
office furniture #2
storage furnite
shelving
counter furniture
disable people counter furniture
seat

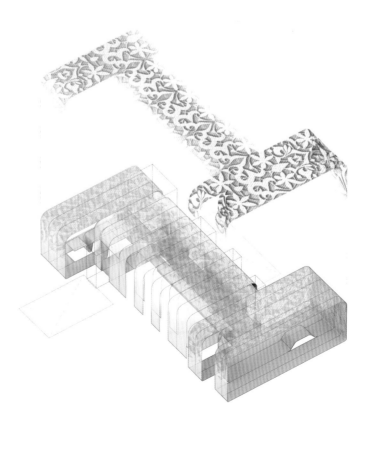

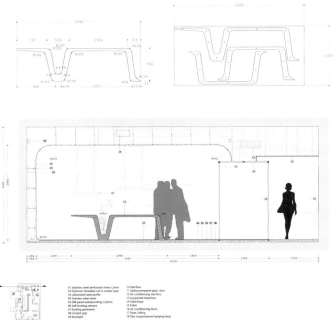

01 Stainless steel perforated sheet 1.2mm
02 Fasteners threaded rod or similar type
03 Galvanized steel profile
04 Stainless steel profile
05 DM panel waterproofing 1.22mm
06 Self leveling cement
07 Existing pavement
08 Cement grip
09 Backlight
10 Oak floor
11 Sliding tempered glass door
12 Air conditioning machine
13 Lacquered metal box
14 Toilet foyer
15 Toilet
16 Air conditioning ducts
17 False Ceiling
18 Tato Suspensione hanging lamp

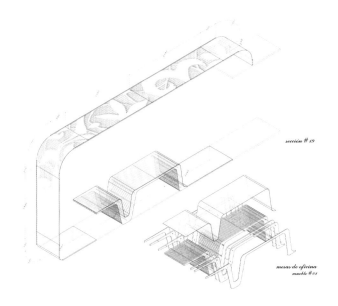

sección # 19

mesas de oficina
mueble # 01

Design | Studiofibre
Client | Agent Provocateur
Photography | @Studiofibre / Pantling Studios
Area | 17,000 sqft
Location | London, UK

Agent Provocateur office

A nod to Agent Provocateur's unique in-store design is reflected throughout the interior through the careful selection of certain key elements. The bespoke black and pink carpets in the meeting rooms, the pink and red Chinese lanterns mixed with black fringed ceiling lampshades and the opulent silk pencil pleat silver curtains with pink motifs soften the space and make it feel more like a "boudoir" and less corporate.

Larger than life posters of the company's product are added to transfer perfectly from store to office. Lip seating and pink fluorescent lighting add fun to the office environment.

Even the back office space of the accounting department doesn't escape the fuschia and shocking pink touches added to the desktop and desk chair coverings.

All the lifts were replaced with a polished finish because the client didn't want brushed stainless steel. A bespoke partitioning system with black metal framework was designed by Studiofibre and rolled out throughout the interior. The restrooms didn't escape the "boudoir" treatment either, with an eclectic mix of ornate sinks, taps and mirrors set against bespoke Agent Provocateur wallpaper and bold black gloss floor and wall tiles.

The roof terrace holds a deck and huge sliding doors give access to an enclosed rooftop cafe and relaxation area, creating a very flexible space perfect for events.

Design | Iosa Ghini Associati Srl
Client | IBM Italia
Photography | Santi Caleca
Area | 1,500 sqm
Location | Rome, Italy

IBM Software Executive Briefing Center

IBM Software Executive Briefing Center in Rome has been entirely renovated and has significantly expanded its area. The entire project, designed by Massimo Iosa Ghini and his studio, elaborates the famous "strips" of the IBM logo in an innovative and fascinating way.

Audiovisual advanced technologies have been carefully selected to provide guests a comfortable and high value-added experience.

The new Software Executive Briefing Center in Rome is located within the same structure that hosts the international laboratory for the development of the IBM Software Group and provides all the tools to explore IBM's technology and its innovative solutions in one new and exciting atmosphere.

The IBM Software Executive Briefing Program is designed to provide professionally managed events and to maximize the value of time that customers spend in IBM. Any "briefing" usually includes presentations and demonstrations to bring customers in to run events in which they participate. The space encourages listening, discussing and illustrating how the new IBM technologies can be helpful in facing and resolving technical and business issues, leading people away from the traditional concept of communication, to get closer to a place of useful comparison: a new agora.

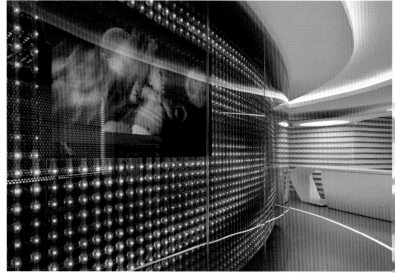

Open Lounge for Raiffeisen

Design | NAU + DGJ
Client | Raiffeisen Bank Schweiz
Photography | Jan Bitter
Area | 400 sqm
Location | Zurich, Switzerland

Raiffeisen's flagship branch on Zurich's Kreuzplatz dissolves traditional barriers between customer and employee, creating a new type of "open bank," a space of encounter. Advanced technologies make banking infrastructure largely invisible; employees access terminals concealed in furniture elements, while a robotic retrieval system grants 24 hour access to safety deposit boxes. This shifts the bank's role into becoming a light-filled, inviting environment – an open lounge where customers can learn about new products and services. Conversations can start spontaneously around a touch-screen equipped info-table and transition to meeting rooms for more private discussions. The info-table not only displays figures from world markets in real-time, but can be used to interactively discover the history of Hottingen, or just check the latest sports scores.

Elegantly flowing walls blend the different areas of the bank into one smooth continuum, spanning from the customer reception at the front, to employee workstations oriented to the courtyard. The plan carefully controls views to create different grades of privacy and to maximize daylight throughout. The walls themselves act as a membrane mediating between the open public spaces and intimately scaled conference rooms. Portraits of the quarter's most prominent past residents like Böklin, Semper or Sypri grace the walls, their abstracted images milled into Hi-macs using advanced digital production techniques. While intricately decorative, the design grounds the bank in the area's cultural past, while looking clearly towards the future.

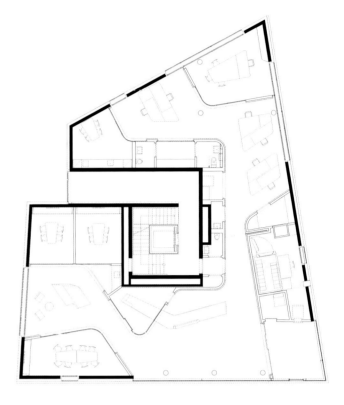

Snowcrash office and showroom

Design | Tham & Videgård Arkitekter
Client | Snowcrash
Photography | Åke E:son Lindman
Area | 1,124 sqm
Location | Stockholm, Sweden

The office layout combines an effective open office with defined rooms of various sizes. The aim is to create an optimum work environment, and aspects such as acoustics, lighting and quality of air were studied separately. The main design element is a continuous, free form glass wall inserted into the existing warehouse structure. By twisting and turning, the glass enclosure generates spaces of different moods, creating unexpected, landscape-like situations and views. The glass panes are all the same size, 1.8x2.4m, and screen printed with a pattern in order to provide a precise visual function and spatial effect. The result is a spatial experiment where the undulating glass core creates defined places within the premises: showroom, east office, kitchen, west office. Simultaneously it constitutes a link between all areas, both visually and logistically.

Since no doors are placed in the glass facing the open office, the amount of accessible free wall surface space is increased and the risk of disturbance between meeting rooms and offices is minimized. As a result a visual and spatial pause is created (as a buffer) in the transition from workspace to meeting space. Deep grey in the passageways underlines this spatial contrast. The color scheme is otherwise atelier-like; with light, neutral tones.

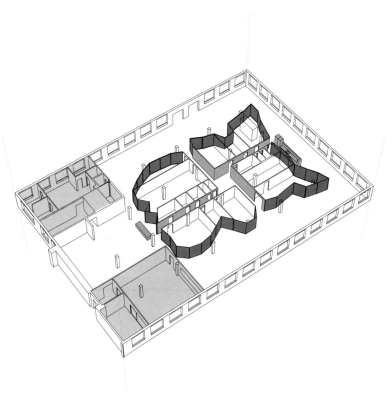

1. ENTRANCE
2. SHOWROOM
3. RECEPTION
4. COPY / PRINTER
5. STORAGE
6. TELEPHONE BOTH
7. STORAGE
8. PROTOTYPE ATELIER
9. WORKSHOP
10. PROJECT- MEETING ROOM
11. OFFICE: DEVELOPMENT
12. OFFICE: ADMINISTRATION
13. KITCHEN
14. MEETING
15. OFFICE: ART & TECHNOLOGY
16. LIVING
17. KITCHENETTE
18. SLEEPING
19. COMPUTER ROOM
20. CLOUD

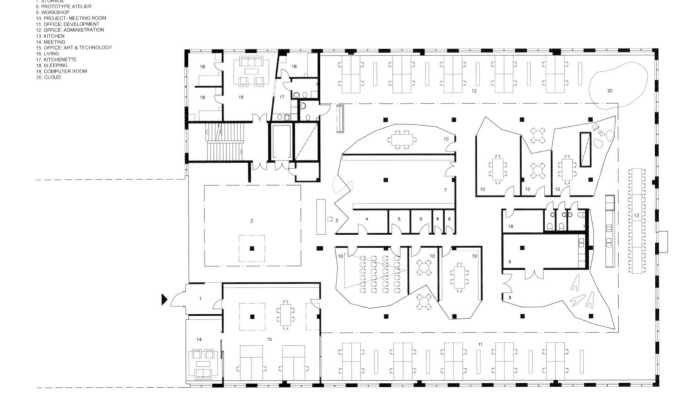

Design | Studiofibre
Client | Net A Porter
Photography | @Studiofibre / Pantling Studios
Area | 44,000 sqft
Location | London, UK

Net A Porter office

Studiofibre transformed a very contemporary, almost industrial shell originally intended for a leisure centre into a 40,000 square foot workplace wonderland with smooth vaulted fabric ceilings, bespoke contemporary lighting rafts, elegant Murano glass chandeliers, soaring oversized paneled doors and a mixture of matte and high gloss finishes that scoop out dimensionality in an otherwise flat, monochromatic palette. The beautifully sculpted bespoke furniture pieces were designed and commissioned by Studiofibre, who also sourced and supplied all of the contract furniture from the desks to the chairs to the more specialist pieces, a savvy concoction of high-end and high street always taking into account the sensible budget constraints whilst choosing the most appropriate and stylish products to dress the stunning interior space.

Structurally, two new mezzanine floors were created, each with its own bold statement staircase, whilst a seamless glass meeting room floats at the entrance to the main hall offering fantastic panoramic views across the working landscape and a vast wooden sculpture of steps sets the scene for the dramatic "Theatre" area at the heart of the space.

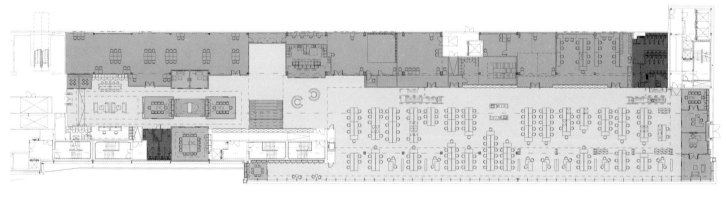
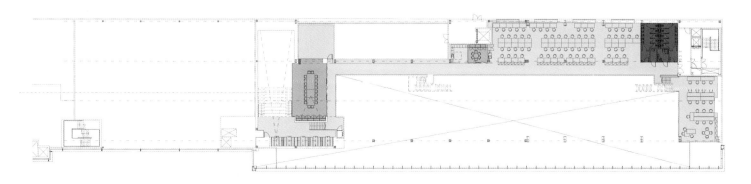

Design | Alexey Kuzmin
Client | Bank of Moscow
Photography | Alexey Knyazev
Area | 7,000 sqm
Location | Moscow, Russia

Bank of Moscow office

The bank's interior representational zones are respectable and rigorous, in their own luxury. Walls and ceilings are decorated with oak panels, the figure from whom the architect has borrowed in the façade. The scheme of the ceiling was created in response to the drawing on the walls. The central hall has the shape of a hexagon; there weren't originally any windows but a diamond-shaped skylight of stained glass was added.

In each wing originally there were three large halls, connected together with a wide and high aperture, so these halls looked like a single space. All necessary zones for staff are divided by glass, so the openings turned into beautifully glazed wooden arches.

At the second level, in the area of personnel, the architect decided not to make design reference to a false history. Instead, a high-tech, comfortable, and modern office was created, with a lot of open space that allows more efficient use of space and natural lighting. A Mansard ceiling was made from acoustic, fire-resistant panels covered with birch veneer sheets.

Design | SHH
Client | Private client
Photography | Alastair Lever
Area | 9,500 sqft
Location | London, UK

Offices for International Shipping Company

This is an office interior project for an international shipping company, set within a 5-storey early Georgian terrace in the West End of London. The new offices are spacious and dramatic, with cool, contemporary furniture and interventions creating a strong contrast with the building's classic fabric, which was renovated as part of the scheme. Major new design features include a bespoke chandelier hanging right through the three storey stair void; new bespoke furniture designed by SHH and beautiful American black walnut

herringbone timber flooring, installed to restore some of the long-lost richness and quality suggested by the original building envelope.

The existing building was really quite dilapidated. Although it had served as office space previously, interventions by previous tenants had been of poor quality, from laminate flooring to dull lighting. SHH therefore sought to pay the building shell a little more respect and also to follow the client's "pure and clean" brief and preference for dark colors, building up a clean, monochrome

material palette. Inevitably, a large slice of the budget also went into the hidden elements necessary to make the offices function to today's standards, including a major upgrade of services, from new data cabling and electrical infrastructure, to air conditioning and fresh air supplies.

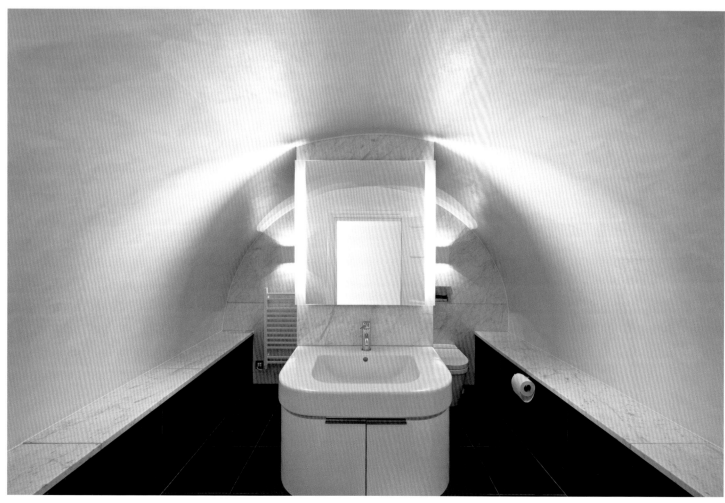

Design I COORDINATION Asia
Client I COORDINATION Asia
Photography I COORDINATION Asia
Area I 350 sqm
Location I Shanghai, China

Huangpi Rd Office

After two successful years at Shanghai's Premium Creative Park M50 (Moganshan Road 50), COORDINATION Asia decided to move somewhere more downtown. They followed the invitation of the Shanghai Glass Company to fill their former headquarters with life until the building will be entirely renovated at the end of 2012. COORDINATION Asia is happy to have now more than 300 sqms of creative space with expanded meeting and presentation facilities.

Huangpi Road 688 is the former headquarters of the Shanghai Glass Company and was initially decorated in the late 90s in a posh European style equipped with fine marble and waxed hardwood floors. All walls are equipped with build-in bookshelves, hidden cabinets, and secret compartments. Reddish Real wood dominated the shabby but somehow classy atmosphere. The ceiling is overloaded with stucco and French style chandeliers.

COORDINATION Asia then dipped the whole floor into a decent grey and pitch black paint pot. Tables with black glass tops and arty photographs of COORDINATION's cradle and hometown Berlin, became the right counterpart to the posh and somehow royal interior.

Design | SHH
Client | Private client
Photography | James Silverman,
Francesca Yorke
Area | 760 sqm
Location | London, UK

Manchester Square

An office interiors scheme for a Russian Investment Company in London's west end, the Manchester Square offices are the result of a brief to create a "high impact, 21st century office interior with a strong personality" with more in common with a gentlemen's club than a traditional office space.

Although the property was made up of a classic (and Grade II-listed) 5-storey Georgian townhouse, with a former stables and garage building to the rear, the client was very open to a sense of contrast for the scheme, favouring a highly contemporary treatment. The inherited interior – also previously an office – was not particularly grand, but any standout details were to be retained, such as marble mosaic floor in the entrance area, a number of marble-inlaid fireplaces and highly detailed ceiling cornicing.

The newly generous per capita space was exploited with very individual rooms with differing color saturation and differing degrees of formality – from a break room to office space to dramatic meeting spaces. The scheme had to house five company directors and around 20 administrative employees, along with meeting facilities, ranging from a formal space on the ground floor to a video-conferencing room and less formal second floor meeting space, as well as a break room.

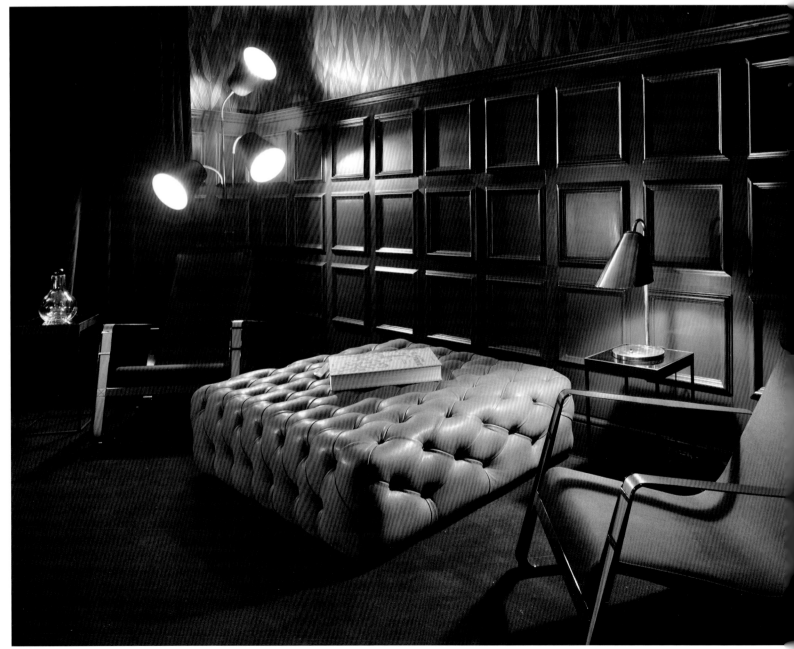

INDEX

Dom Arquitectura, Spain

www.dom-arquitectura.com

We understand each project as a different challenge, we try to innovate, experiment and learn from each one. We especially like the relationship with their environment, urban or natural. Integrate it into the site, flow with your feelings and perceptions of our intense look on the nature of the place, gives us the basis to define each project.

We enjoy architecture as if it were a game. It involves the management of light, shape, materials and the creative process. The strong finish is what makes us happy and so we work hard everyday.

p060-063

Electric Dreams, Sweden

www.electricdreams.se

Electric Dreams is a Stockholm-based architecture/design studio formed by Joel Degermark and Catharina Frankander in 2006. Joel is a product designer trained at the Royal College of Art, London and Beckmans School of Design, Stockholm. Catharina is an architect trained at the Architectural Association, London, and Royal Institute of Technology, Stockholm.

We specialize in brand environments and products. Our designs are much about story-telling and themes, a fascination of playful exaggeration. We like things that are too colorful, too weird, too beautiful, too dark, too many… Our design is a lot about shifting scales, bringing two familiar things together to create the unfamiliar, and playing with visual effects.

p098-101

elisavalero, Spain

www.elisavalero.com

I am interested in living space, landscape, sustainability, precision and an economy of expressive resources. I am interested in architecture rooted in the earth and in its own time. I accept the determinants of architecture as the rules of a very serious and enjoyable game and I try to play it in a coherent, rigorous way.

While it is no longer stylish to speak of serving, I believe that an architect's work is a quintessential service intended to make people's lives more agreeable – a noble calling that seeks to make the world more beautiful and more human and to make society fairer. Architecture is not for the nostalgic. It is a job for rebels.

124-127

Estudio Mytaki, Spain

www.mytaki.es

Estudio Mytaki was formed in 2006 in response to collective concerns related to architecture and its intersection with other associated disciplines. This reaction causes an open work space, understood as a common place of learning and enrichment, to develop our professional activity. At present, our study in Granada is composed of six architects, two students of architecture and a large group of collaborators. The uncertain labor situation around us affects our industry and at the same time motivates us to work and be creative against this development gap.

Estudio Mytaki is an open office professionals developing different lines, projects and competitions from the architectural scale to the urban rehabilitation, interior design and exhibition stands, advisory services, technical reports, 3D computer graphics and graphic design.

p214-217

FORM US WITH LOVE design studio, Sweden

www.formuswithlove.se

FORM US WITH LOVE is a design studio operating in Stockholm. The internationally acclaimed studio was started in 2005 by the trio of Jonas Pettersson, John Löfgren and Petrus Palmér. FORM US WITH LOVE aims to challenge the conventional through design initiatives.

FUWL partners with companies which involves in the development and production of everyday objects, furniture and lighting.

p008-009

HASSELL, Australia

www.hassell.com.au

HASSELL is one of the world's largest privately owned design-based practices, with a network of 12 studios located throughout Asia and Australia.

Each HASSELL studio has the flexibility and independence to tailor high quality services to meet the needs of local clients while also accessing the combined resources and collective international experience of the practice as a whole – bringing the very best talent to every project team.

Our designers work collaboratively within a multidisciplinary team that includes architects, interior designers, landscape architects, planners, urban designers and experts in sustainable design.

p148-151, p152-157

i29 interior architects, the Netherlands

www.i29.nl

We are Jaspar Jansen (1970) and Jeroen Dellensen (1972). In 2001 we joined forces and a year later i29 I interior architects was born, a creative and versatile interior design studio.

Our aim is to create intelligent designs and striking images. Space is the leitmotiv, the result is always clear, with a keen eye for detail.

Our approach is practical yet based on strong ideas articulated in clear concepts. We try to get to the core of things but keep it simple.

p024-027

Iosa Ghini Associati Srl, Italy

www.iosaghini.it

Born in 1959, Massimo Iosa Ghini studied architecture in Florence and then graduated from Polytechnic Institute of Milan. Today he is considered one of the best known Italian architects and designers on the international scene.

His works can be found in various museums and private collections. His projects have received important international awards, including the Roscoe Award USA, 1988, the Good Design Award in 2001, 2004, 2009 and 2010 by the Chicago Athenaeum and the Red Dot Award in 2003.

p222-227

Ippolito Fleitz Group, Germany

www.ifgroup.org

Ippolito Fleitz Group is a multidisciplinary, internationally operating design studio based in Stuttgart. We are identity architects. We work in unison with our clients to develop architecture, products and communication that are part of a whole and yet distinctive in their own right. This is how we define identity.

As architects of identity, we conceive and construct buildings, interiors and landscapes; we develop products and communication measures. We do not think in disciplines. We think in solutions.

p106-111, p138-143

Jackie-B, Denmark

www.jackie-b.com

Jackie-B: Interior architect and furniture designer.

Jackie-B specializes in creative workspace and interior design where design is given the right to create experiences and bring the companies' practical realities into form.

The office's approach is always to let the key essence in the clients' vision be a vital player in bringing out a concept where now is yesterday. A new designed spatial work as a tool get the client's vision adjusted from speaking to doing.

The office is centrally located in Vesterbro in Copenhagen, Denmark.

p128-131

Jos Roodbol, the Netherlands

www.josroodbol.nl

Jos Roodbol (1959) studied architecture at the faculty of Bouwkunde in Delft (1977-1984) and lived and worked in Paris (1982-1983) and Tokyo (1984-1986). His studio is based in Amsterdam. To be able to execute projects of different scales he works together with other disciplines: architects, landscape, architects and urban planners.

p010-013

Kamat & Rozario Architecture, India

www.kamatrozario.com

Kamat & Rozario Architecture was set up in 2007 in Bangalore. We are currently active in the fields of architecture, interiors & furniture design, but the possibilities are endless. Our endeavor is always to put forward simple, yet strong ideas. We believe that each project and each client is unique and for this reason, each design must also be unique.

p048-051

Lehrer Architects, US

www.lehrerarchitects.com

Smart, modern designs from Lehrer Architects fuse effortless beauty and keen perspective into internationally acclaimed works of art. Founded in 1985 by Michael B. Lehrer, FAIA, the Los Angeles firm crafts dynamic spaces nationwide, while maintaining its hometown roots. From the intimate to the monumental, the firm's work is grounded in the idea that beauty is a rudiment of human dignity. The architects revere light and space as the spiritual essence of architecture.

p118-121

Marcos Samaniego / MAS ARQUITECTURA, Spain

www.mas.es

Versatile, creative and innovative capacity, Marcos Samaniego Reimíndez (A Coruña, 1971), offers a refreshing vision of architecture. He is able to link natural resources and cultural heritage. His contact with European culture and design, during his formative stage in Barcelona, has accentuated his professional personality: details and the spaces have a particular goal, away from the impersonality.

His designs have been featured in international publications, as well as in newspapers and magazines. The combination of tradition and design is highlighted by experts, who consider Marcos Samaniego one of the great promises of Spanish architecture.

p204-209

Mathieu Lehanneur, France

www.mathieulehanneur.com

A graduate from L'ENSCI – Les Ateliers in 2001, Mathieu Lehanneur founded in the same year his own design and interior design studio. He has a passion for early interactions between the body and its environment, living systems and the scientific world. Mixing his creations with technology and natural elements, he develops and explores design projects in the pharmaceutical, biological or astrophysics world.

p042-047

Maurice Mentjens Design, the Netherlands

www.mauricementjens.com

Maurice Mentjens primarily designs interiors and related objects and furnishings. Creations are almost exclusively for the project sector: shops, hotels and restaurants, offices and museums. Intriguing, smaller scale projects are preferred to larger projects. The aim of this compact, talented and dynamic team is to deliver high-end design reflecting its passion. Quality and creativity are prioritized in all aspects of the design and implementation process. The agency is three times winner of the Dutch Design Award. In 2007, the design agency received the Design Award of the Federal Republic of Germany.

p144-147

MMASA Studio, Spain

http://mmasastudio.wordpress.com

MMASA Studio was set up in 2004 by Patricia Muñiz (1974) and Luciano G. Alfaya (1974), architects from the Universidade da Coruña. From the Andar Quatro group, they work on different areas to raise awareness of architectural activities.

Their architectural activities combine both institutional and private works. Their residential projects have focused on research in single-family houses. They have been awarded a number of prizes in national competitions, among which the first prize for the new Almagro courthouse in Ciudad Real or the Palace of Justice in O Barco de Valdeorras stand out.

p210-213

mode:lina architektura & consulting, Poland

www.modelina-architekci.com

mode:lina was founded by Paweł Garus and Jerzy Woźniak in 2009 in Poznań, both formerly members of Rotterdam-based architectural practice 123DV.

mode:lina is a group of designers specializing in

creation of space and design, whose passion is creating beautiful things, while fully functional and environmentally friendly. When designing we strive to create a space that reflects the individual style of life and ensuring maximum impression.

mode:lina has the highest quality, out-of-the-box thinking, attention to detail, professional advice and close cooperation with both our clients and specialists.

p132-133

NAU, Germany

www.nau.coop

NAU is an international, multidisciplinary design firm, spanning the spectrum from architecture and interior design to exhibitions and interactive interfaces. They have offices in Zurich, Berlin, and Los Angeles. As futurists creating both visual design and constructed projects, NAU melds the precision of experienced builders with the imagination and attention to detail required to create innovative exhibitions, public events and architecture. NAU has quickly garnered recognition as an accomplished creator of fashionable interiors for retail, hotels, restaurants and residences. Its dedicated teams offer a personal touch, working with clients to align design approach with the appropriate market. Distilled in clear, contemporary forms, the designs of NAU promote modern, flexible solutions that are engaging and welcoming.

p228-231

nendo, Japan

www.nendo.jp

Giving people a small "!" moment.

There are so many small "!" moments hidden in our everyday lives, but we don't always recognize them. But we believe these small "!" moments are what make our days so interesting and rich – which is why we want to reconstitute the everyday by collecting and reshaping unique moments of inspiration into something that's easy to understand.

We'd like the people who've encountered nendo's designs to feel these small "!" moments intuitively.

That's nendo's job.

p014-015

Origins Architecture, the Netherlands

www.origins-architecten.nl

Origins Architecture is an architectural office based in Rotterdam. The office specializes in environmental-friendly and energy-efficient building.

Origins Architecture was founded by architect Jamie van Lede, on the premise that sustainable building can and should be inspiring and self-evident in order to succeed. The office works from the principle that consideration of environmental aspects in the design process creates added value.

Over the years, the office has successfully combined esthetical and sustainable qualities in award-winning projects. 1+1 sometimes equals 3 and it's the office's ambition to keep on demonstrating this in the built environment.

p016-019

PS Arkitektur, Sweden
www.psarkitektur.com/projekt.php

We enhance our clients' image and business capacity through innovative architecture and design. Our motto is Architecture for change.

We work with a broad range of projects ranging from urban planning to buildings and commercial interiors. Our aim is to create unique buildings and interiors that speak for themselves.

We reveal the potential, visualize the hidden and suggest improvements. Architecture and design is a means of competition that creates withstanding value. In cooperation with the client we define the specifications and goals of the project in order to create a design that communicates and strengthens the client's identity.

p102-105, p112-117

Rios Clementi Hale Studios, US
www.rchstudios.com

Rios Clementi Hale Studios, established in 1985, has developed an international reputation for its collaborative and multidisciplinary approach, establishing an award-winning tradition across an unprecedented range of design disciplines. Acknowledging the firm's varied body of work, the American Institute of Architects California Council gave Rios Clementi Hale Studios its 2007 Firm Award, the organization's highest honor. For its varied landscape work – from civic parks to private gardens – the firm was named a finalist in the 2009 National Design Awards. The architecture, landscape architecture, planning, urban, interior, exhibition, graphic, and product designers at Rios Clementi Hale Studios create buildings, places, and products that are thoughtful, effective, and beautiful.

p070-073

SELGASCANO, Spain
www.selgascano.net

SELGASCANO works in Madrid. It is a small studio and it's their intention to remain so. They have never taught at any university and they don't tend to give lectures in order to focus intensely on projects. They

centre their work on the construction process, treating it as a continuous listening to the largest possible number of elements involved on it from manufacture to installation.

They have exhibited at the MOMA in NY, the Guggenheim in NY, the Venice Biennale and the GA Gallery in Tokyo.

p122-123

Sergey Makhno, Ukraine
www.mahno.com.ua

Sergey Makhno is an artist, architect, designer, workshop project manager. In 1999 he founded "Makhno workshop". Sergey believes that his imaginative vision is the combination of contradictory backgrounds and creation of artistic mixes from seemingly incompatible things. He prefers rather not to have a rest but pay a visit to world design exhibitions and into antique shops, where he may come up with an invention and devise not only well-forgotten old things but also new ones that are never thought of before. Apart from interiors, he designs original furniture, produces pictures, collages, collects antique suitcases, eau-fortes, towels, radio-phonographs, and scissors.

p092-093

SHH, UK
www.shh.co.uk

Brendan Heath is an Associate at SHH, who joined the company in 2003 after working in the UK and Sydney, where he studied Interior Design. Brendan has worked on numerous residential and restaurant projects at SHH, as well as a number of outstanding office schemes, including the Farnborough Demo Lab (shortlisted for a Lighting Design Award) and the Manchester Square offices in central London, which won the ICIAD Silver Grand Award in 2008 in China; the Interior Design Award (UK Property Awards); the Best Workplace Award (FX International Interior Design Awards) and the International Interior Design Award (International Property Awards in San Diego).

p248-253, p258-265

SPACE, Mexico
www.spacemex.com

Not long ago SPACE was opened with the intention of working with corporations which think that space makes a difference. Our passion has always been design and architecture. We structure a new way of seeing architecture and we develop methodologies inline with this vision.

With an interest in being the best if not the biggest, we surround ourselves with an interdisciplinary team of highly talented professionals.

We take into account the importance of research and technology and we include both in our method of thinking and working, always seeking SUSTAINABLE solutions which not only RESPECT the environment but also help to improve our surroundings.

p158-161, p162-165, p166-171, p172-177

Studio BA, Israel
www.studioba.co.il

Studio BA is a vibrant and visionary design team located in the heart of Tel Aviv. Managed by the Industrial Designer Omri Amoyal and the Architect Moran Ben Hur, the studio specializes in contemporary commercial spaces. As a team, we conceptualize the project out of an empowerment of collaborative ideas. These ideas are based on factors such as; product concept, client needs, budget and time of implementation.

We challenge ourselves daily and bring with it the passion and enthusiasm that is evident in our design, craftsmanship and commitment to our final goal of client's satisfaction.

p064-069

Studio Joost van Bleiswijk, the Netherlands
www.projectjoost.com

Joost van Bleiswijk was born in Delft, 1976. He graduated from the Design Academy Eindhoven in 2001 and got lots of reviews with his "outlines" series. His work is sold and exhibited through international galleries including Moss gallery, New York and Vivid gallery, Rotterdam and international museums such as the Holon Design Museum in Israel and the Zuiderzeemuseum in the Netherlands.

Craftsmanship and traditional techniques are important to Joost. He chooses to work not only with sustainable materials, but also with products that have an everlasting and timeless image.

p020-023

Studiofibre, UK
www.studiofibre.com

Studiofibre is a multidisciplinary design company based in the Chiltern Hills, northwest of London. It is established in 2007 by Fiona and Ian Livingston, who provide over 30 years of creative experience in the design industry. Studiofibre is today a vibrant, evolving design studio with a portfolio of projects that encompass a broad range of sectors.

The company's philosophy emphasizes the creativity of thought and the pursuit of a "non-style" through and the notion that every design solution derives itself from the micro-specifics of a particular brief, site context and budget, mixed with the macro-specifics of a wide social and cultural setting.

p218-221, p238-243

studioquint, the Netherlands

www.studioquint.com

Oliver Ebben (1970) studied architecture in Münster, Germany. As an architect he gained work experience at the two Amsterdam-based offices Claus en Kaan and VMX architects. In 2005 he founded his own office studioquint. He also teaches at the department of architecture at TU Delft.

p010-013

TERVHIVATAL, Hungary

www.tervhivatal.hu

Young Hungarian architects Zsanett BENEDEK and Dániel LAKOS established the architectural and design studio called TERVHIVATAL in 2008. Their profile ranges from architecture to object design. Their goal is to give the most suitable answer to every upcoming problem, either the restoration on a flooded area or design a new door handle.

p034-037

Tham & Videgård Arkitekter, Sweden

www.tvark.se

Tham & Videgård Arkitekter is a progressive and contemporary practice that focuses on architecture and design – from large scale urban planning through to buildings, interiors and objects.

The practice's objective is to create distinct and relevant architecture with the starting point resting within the unique context and specific conditions of the individual project. Taking an active approach, the office is involved throughout the whole process, from developing the early sketch to on-site supervision. Commissions include public, commercial and private clients in Sweden and abroad.

p232-237

upsetters architects, Japan

www.upsetters.jp

"Observe the city and reconstruct the cityscape"

Declaring this as our concept, we are working interdisciplinary on architecture, interior design, events, and etc which are related to all city activities.

We are awarded JCD Design Award Gold Prize, Good Design Awards, and so on.

p134-137

za bor architects, Russia

www.zabor.net

za bor is a Moscow-based architectural office founded in 2003 by principals Arseniy Borisenko and Peter Zaytsev.

The bureau's projects are created mainly in contemporary aesthetic. What distinguishes them is an abundance of architectural methods used both in the architectural and interior design, as well as a complex dynamic shape which is a signature style of za bor projects. The interiors demonstrate this feature especially brightly, since for all their objects Peter and Arseniy create built-in and free standing furniture themselves.

p052-055, p178-181, p198-203

ACKNOWLEDGEMENTS

We would like to thank all the designers for their kind permission to publish their outstanding office design projects. Our thanks also go to all of the photographers, writers, and PR people who have given us great support and assistance. Without them we would not be able to share these amazing projects to readers around the world.